MW01618451

CHAPTER TWELVE

Utopic Degeneration: Disneyland

PROPOSITION:

A degenerate utopia is ideology changed into the form of a myth.

REFERENCES:

1. Ideology is the representation of the imaginary relationship individuals maintain with their real conditions of existence.
2. Utopia is an ideological place; utopia is a sort of ideological discourse.
3. Utopia is an ideological place where ideology is put into play; it is a stage for ideological representation.
4. Myth is a narrative that resolves formally a fundamental social contradiction.

COMMENTARY:

In trying to analyze Disneyland as a utopic space, two goals are intended. First, I mean to show the permanence of some patterns of spatial organization that can be qualified as utopic. Not only can they be found in architectural schemata and related works, but they are also in works that fill a specific function with regard to reality, history, and social relations. The patterns I am seeking can all be classed, theoretically and speculatively, as expressions of utopic practice. All contain a neutralizing critical impact, and within ideology the neutralization defines the specific space for building and elaborating social theory. These patterns and functions appear in the topography of a real space in California, and by the visitor's real use of it. From this vantage point the even-

[illegible] commence when they come to Disneyland can be viewed [illegible] that characterizes utopia. The map of Disneyland visitors buy in [illegible] how to go from one place to another can play the role of the [illegible] performs the part of the representational picture which also [illegible] utopia. But this real example is more interesting from another [illegible]iew: I would like to show how a utopic structure and utopic functions [illegible]ate, how the utopic representation can be entirely caught in a dominant [illegible] of ideas and values and, thus, be changed into a myth or a collective [illegible]asy.

Disneyland is the representation realized in a geographical space of the imaginary relationship that the dominant groups of American society maintain with their real conditions of existence, with the real history of the United States, and with the space outside of its borders. Disneyland is a fantasmatic projection of the history of the American nation, of the way in which this history was conceived with regard to other peoples and to the natural world. Disneyland is an immense and displaced metaphor of the system of representations and values unique to American society.

This function has an obvious ideological function. It alienates the visitor by a distorted and fantasmatic representation of daily life, by a fascinating image of the past and the future, of what is estranged and what is familiar: comfort, welfare, consumption, scientific and technological progress, superpower, and morality. These are values obtained by violence and exploitation; here they are projected under the auspices of law and order.

All ideological pressures are brought to the fore here. All the forms and aspects of capitalist alienation and of modern imperialism are represented. Disneyland is the representation of the makeup of contemporary American ideology. Because this place is a stage and place of projection where we can view and test out the ideology of the dominant groups in American society, we might assume that this world built by Walt Disney fulfills the critical function for ideology we noted for utopic production in general.

This is not the case, however, because this "stage" where ideology is put into play and where its critical function comes to operate is really not a stage. The visitors to Disneyland are on stage themselves; they are actors in the performance in which they act. They are captured, like a rat in a maze, and are alienated by their part without being aware of performing a part. In this way, then, Disneyland does not "work" like a projection of ideological representation. Disney's utopia really is not a utopia. Only when a meta-discourse analyzes its map does it become one. Then we can look at the semantic structures. We can

examine how the visitors' tour becomes a narrative, how their itinerary [illegible]

a narrative, how their itinerary becomes "textual," revealing a reading for [illegible] picture as a whole. The divergent systems then emerge, pitted one against the other, and their correlations can be examined. Thus the backstage workings are revealed, and their ideological meanings and repercussions can be pinpointed. It is at this point that a degenerate utopia, changed into text and image, can start to produce. It should tell us what we have known since the development of a theory of political economy and ideology.

In other words, the visitors to Disneyland are put in the place of the ceremonial storyteller. They recite the mythic narrative of the antagonistic origins of society. They go through the contradictions while they visit the complex; they are led from the pirates' cave to an atomic submarine, from Sleeping Beauty's castle to a rocketship. These sets reverse daily life's determinism only to reaffirm it, but legitimated and justified. Their path through the park is the narrative, recounted umpteen times, of the deceptive harmonization of contrary elements, of the fictional solution to conflicting tensions. By "acting out" Disney's utopia, the visitor "realizes" the ideology of America's dominant groups as the mythic founding narrative for their own society.

The Limit

One of the most notable features of the utopic figure is its limit: the utopic discourse inscribes the utopic representation in the imaginary space of a map, but at the same time it makes its inscription in a geographical map impossible. There is an insuperable gap between our world and utopia. This separation is usually indicated by a narrative mark in the signifier. We have seen this, for example, in the manuscript that turns out to be the ship's log of a captain who has visited a utopia. The first pages, which contain the blessed island's precise location, have been removed, however. Another example might be the narrator who has suffered a blow knocking him unconscious, only to wake up once on the marvelous island. As well, a servant could have a violent coughing fit just as our narrator reveals the island's coordinates. A voyage to the Perfect City begins only given this sole condition: this empty abyss must commence the tour. In other words, this signifying mark in the text indicates the image-producing operation in the discourse by signaling its condition of possibility. It corresponds to the semiotic transposition brought about by the frame, using a signifier/signified as a detour.

PASH BUZARI
RAINBOWS IN CURVED AIR

50th Venice Biennial - Utopia Station

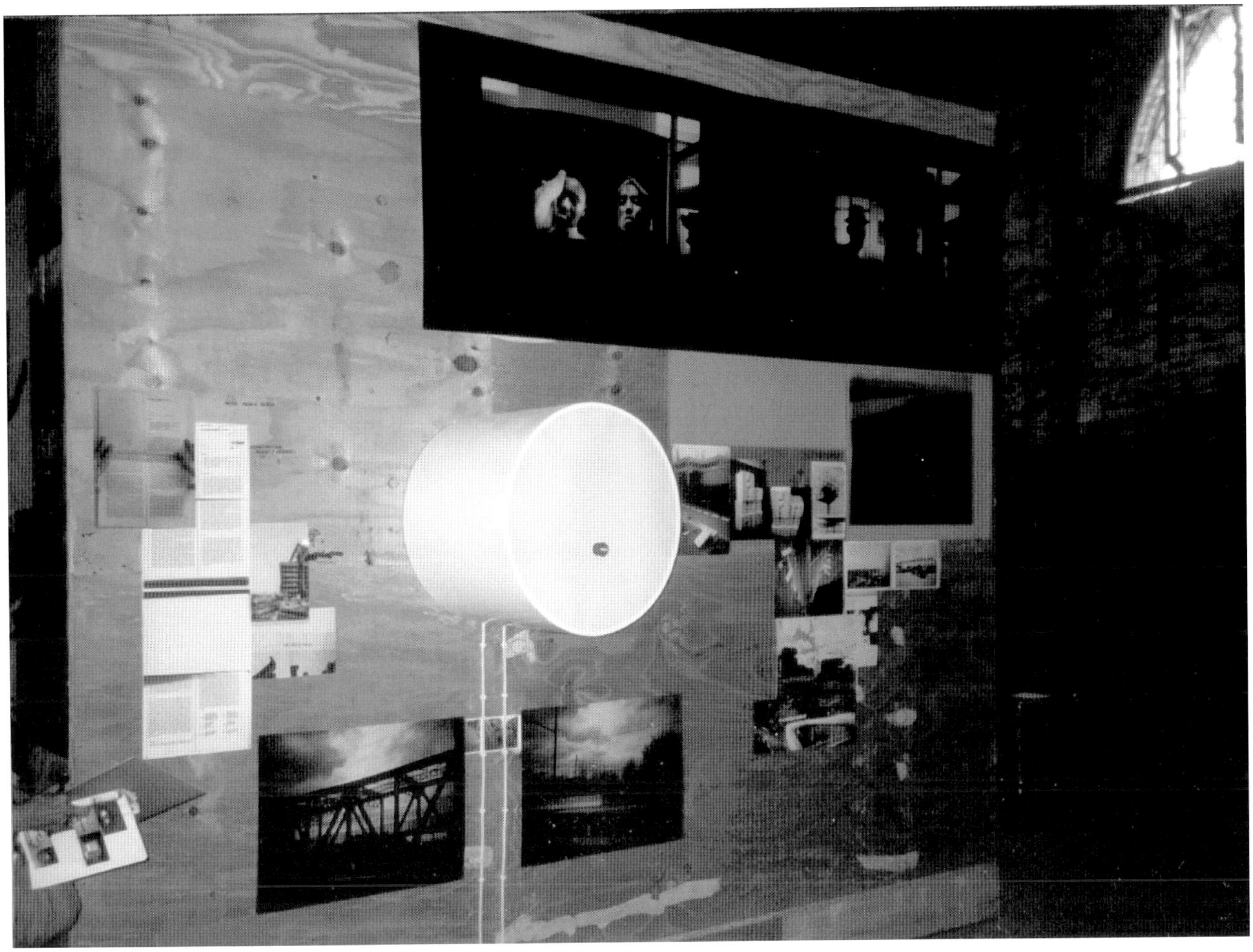

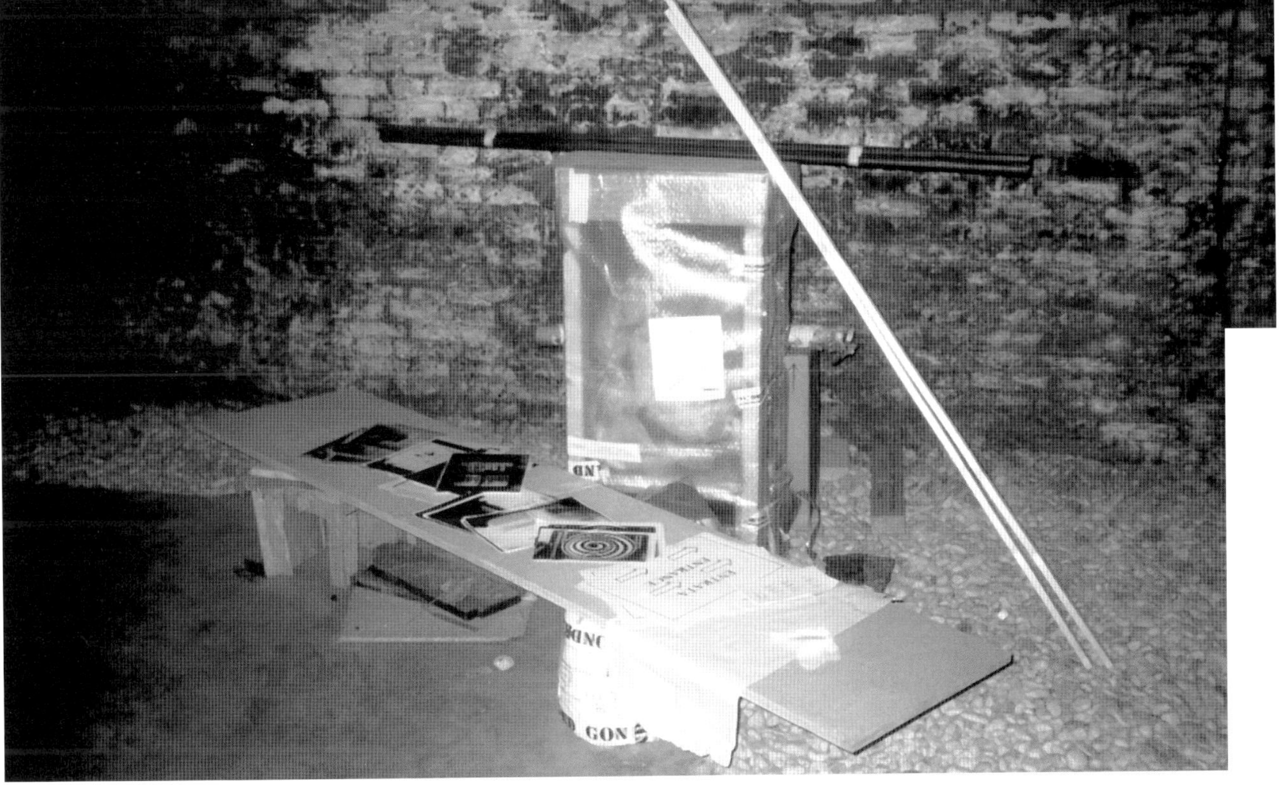

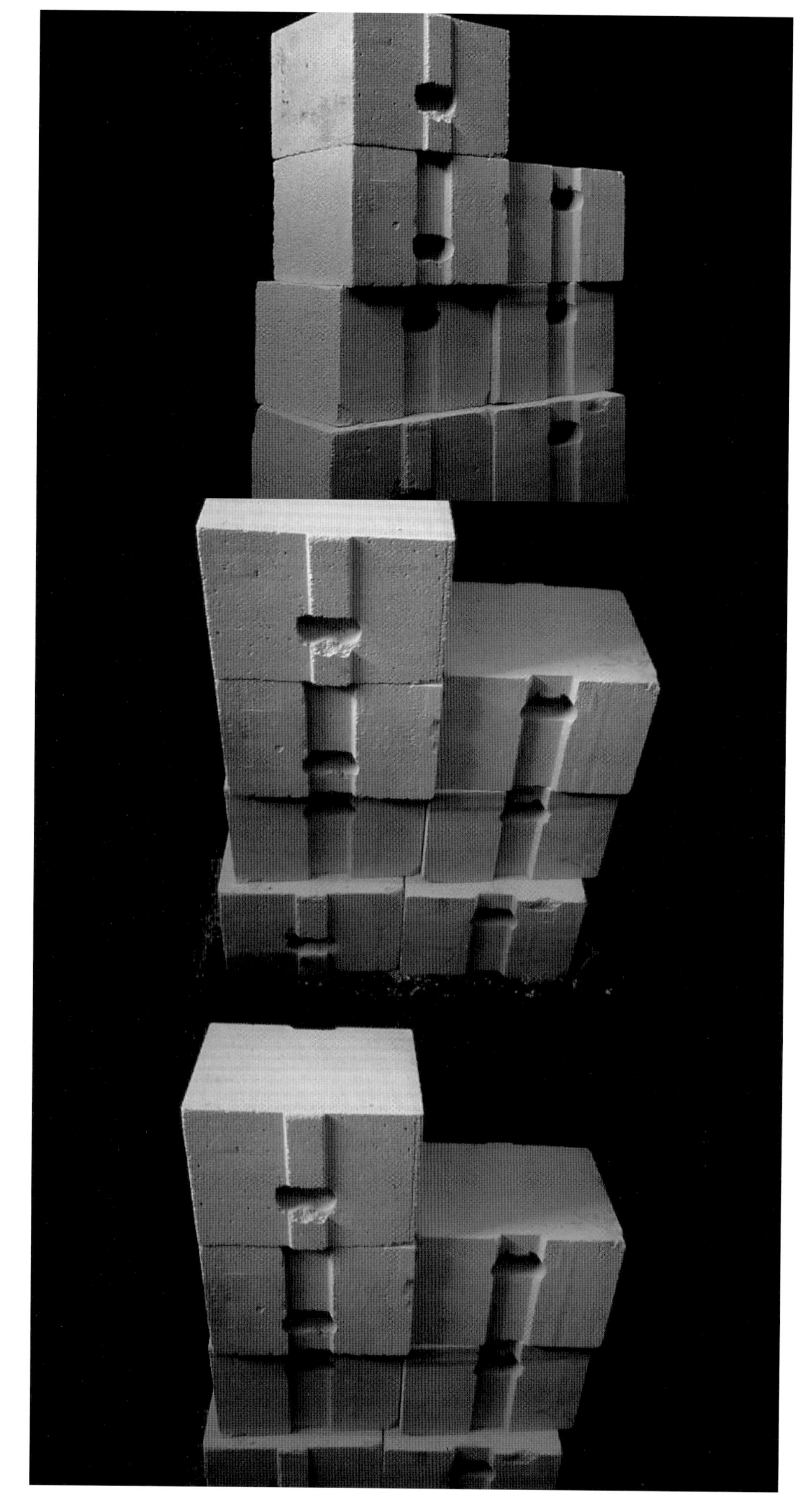

...Politics of Spatiality

Now, the argument here is that this approach to the conceptualisation of space/spatiality resonates with recent shifts in certain quarters in the way in which 'progressive' politics can also be imagined. Although it would be incorrect, and too rigidly constraining, to propose any simple one to one mapping, it is nonetheless the case that each of the three propositions advanced above elucidates a slightly different aspect of this connection. Thus:

i. imagining space as a product of interrelationships (proposition one) chimes well with the emergence over recent years of a politics which attempts to operate through a commitment to anti-essentialism. That is, in place of a kind of identity politics which takes those identities as already, and for ever, constituted ('woman', 'homosexual'), and argues for the rights of, or claims to equality for, those already-constituted identities, this anti-essentialist politics takes the constitution of the identities themselves to be one of the central stakes of the political. Rather than accepting and working with already-constituted identities, this anti-essentialist politics lays it stress on the constructedness of identities and things (including those things called political subjectivities and political constituencies). It is wary therefore about claims to authenticity based on notions of unchanging identity; instead, it proposes a relational understanding of the world.

This politics of interrelations, mirrors, then, the first proposition of this paper, that space too is a product of interrelations. Indeed more generally I would argue , that identities/entities, the relations 'between' them, and the spatiality which is part of them are all co-constitutive. Chantal Mouffe, in particular, has written very insightfully on how we might conceptualise the relational construction of political subjectivities. For her, identity and interrelation are constituted together. What I am proposing here is that space is necessarily integral to and a product of that process of constitution. Not only, then, is there a parallel between the manner of conceptualising space and the manner of conceptualising entities/identities (such as political subjects) but also space is from the beginning integral to the constitution of those political subjectivities;

ii. further, imagining space as the sphere of the possibility of the existence of multiplicity (proposition two) accords with the greater emphasis which has over recent years in political discourses of the left been laid on 'difference' and multiplicity. Thus in what has been perhaps the most evident form which this has taken, there has been a growing insistence that the story of the world can not be told (nor its geography elaborated) through the eyes of 'The West' alone (as had been so long the case) nor form the viewpoint of, for instance, that classic figure (ironically, frequently itself essentialised) of the white, heterosexual male. This approach insists upon a recognition that these understandings (through the eyes of the West, or the straight male) are themselves specific; quite particular local viewpoints, and not the universals which they have for so long proposed themselves to be. It is an approach which has been elaborated and fought above all by feminists and those working within the framework of postcolonial studies.

The relationship between this aspect of changing politics (and manner of doing social theory) and the second proposition about space is of rather different nature form that in the case of the first proposition. In this case, the argument is that the very possibility of any serious recognition of multiplicity and difference itself depends on a recognition of spatiality. Quite often this recognition will be implicit (sometimes harmlessly so, sometimes with serious detrimental effects); at others, particularly when spatiality is itself one of the dimensions of the construction of difference it will be-must be-explicit. This argument will be taken up again later, but the essence of the case is that for there to be multiplicity (and by extension for there to be difference) there must be space;

iii. finally, imagining space as always in a process of becoming, as never a closed system (proposition three) resonates with an increasingly vocal insistence within political discourses on the genuine openness of the future. It is an insistence founded in an attempt to escape the inexorability which so frequently characterizes the grand narratives related to Modernity. The frameworks of 'Progress', of 'Development' and of 'Modernisation', and the succession of modes of production elaborated within Marxism all propose scenarios in which the general directions of history, including the future, are known. However much it may be necessary to fight to bring them about, to engage in struggles for their achievement, there was always nonetheless a background conviction about the direction in which history was moving. Many theorists today reject such a a formulation and argue instead for a radical openness of the future, whether they argue it through radical democracy , through notions of nomadism or through certain approaches within queer theory Indeed, as Laclau in particular would most strongly argue, only if we conceive of the suture as genuinely open can we seriously accept or engage in any genuine notions of politics.

Now here again-as in the case of the first proposition-there is a parallel with the way in which I am urging that we conceptualise spatiality. Both space and history are 'open'-indeed, as the argument progresses, I hope it will so become evident that these two opennesses are really two sides of the same coin, each essential to the other. Conceptualising space as 'open, unfinished, always becoming', in other words, is an essential pre-requisite for history to be open; and thus, after the arguments of Laclau, a prerequisite for the possibility of politics.

* * *

It may be that on initial reading these propositions about space/spatiality seem unexceptionable; that they seem reasonable and are quite quickly accepted. Ina strange way (although of course I heartily want you –eventually-to agree with me) that might be for me a disappointing response. For I also want to argue that these elements of a revised imagination of space are new, that they in some cases flatly contradict and in other cases serious challenge the customary ways in which we think about space. One aspect of this is, as already mentioned, that we often do not think about space-we use the word, in popular discourse or in academic, without being fully conscious of what we mean by it. Another aspect of the way in which this proposed revision of our imagination of space is a challenge derives from the fact that there have been many conceptualisations which are startlingly different.

So, in this section, in order to underline what is different about the three propositions outlined above, I shall spend just a little time examining some ways in which space has been thought about, and thought about by very significant theorists and school of theory, which are completely different from what is being proposed here. This elaboration of other views will enable a deepening of the argument about the present propositions.

First, there is a long an influential line of thinking within 'Continental philosophy' whose main concern as the fact, in this sphere, with the conceptualisation of time but in whose work this preoccupation with the temporal had as a by-product a highly particular understanding of space. (This connection between conceptualisations of time and conceptualisations of space is not restricted to this group. As we shall see, it is integral to many of the positions which follow. It is also part of my own argument: that the two conceptualisations are (coherently or incoherently) related. IN the present case, as has already been indicated, the argument is that any conceptualisation of time which is radically open requires as its partner a conceptualisation of space, too, as open.) In this first line of thinking Henri Bergson is probably the emblematic figure. His influence remains powerful today, perhaps most especially in the work of Deleuze and Guattari. So this is not 'merely' a historical matter.

The second proposition of this paper is that it is space which is the sphere of the possibility of the existence of multiplicity. By extension space as a dimension is necessary to the existence of difference. This is diametrically opposed to Bergson. For Bergson, it was time which is the essential dimension of difference. The reason for this was what, for Bergson and others including many current theorists, 'difference' was itself imagined, not as a potential aspect of multiplicity as in the paper, but as change in time. The reasons for Bergson's position need not detain us ere, though my own hunch is that they derived from the battle in which this strand of philosophy was engaged with Newtonian and Einsteinian science. The logic, insofar as conceptualisations of space were concerned, was devastating. If difference is defined as change (of one thing in time) (rather than as the simultaneous existence of a multiplicity of things), then time is the crucial dimension of difference, and time becomes the crucial dimension, the sole vehicle, of creativity. Space, therefore, is excluded from any process of creativity (in other words the openness of the future: proposition three). Indeed for Bergson space was the dimension of representation, of fixity, of tying things down. It was the language of scientists rather than (he opposed the two) the life of the world. It was thus that he could write:

We must break out of the spatialisation imposed by mind in order to regain contact with the core of the truly living, which subsist only in the time dimension.

Space, then, as the realm of stasis. Perhaps the most provocative statement by Bergson in this regard is the following:

What is the role of time? …Time prevents everything from being given at once…It is not the vehicle of creativity and choice? Is not the existence of time the proof of indeterminism in nature?

A whole host of points clamor for attention here. To begin with, it should be pointed out that 'indeterminism' in this quotation is meant to mean precisely that creativity and that possibility of politics- that genuine openness of the future (proposition three!) – for which this paper too is arguing. For Bergson, change implied real novelty, the production of the new, of things not already totally determined by the current arrangement of forces. Thus:

To [Bergson] the future is becoming in a way that can never be a mere rearrangement of what has been.

The first point to note, then, is that there is some coincidence of desires here. Both Bergson's project and the argument of the present paper push towards opening up our conceptualisations of temporality and the future,

The second part, however, highlighted the divergences, and these concern our understandings of what is thus required of space and time. In the earlier quotation, Bergson writes that time is the vehicle of change. That much might be conceded. But being the vehicle is not the same as being the cause. Unless one takes a thoroughly essentialist position, time can not somehow unaided bootstraps itself into existence, That is to say, unless one holds to some notion of an immanent unfolding of an undifferentiated entity, only interaction can produce change (creativity) and therefore time. However, the possibility of interaction is dependent upon the prior existence of multiplicity (there must be more than one entity in order for interaction to be possible; the pure form of the argument is of course that the interaction itself is integral to the production of the entities). In other words:

* for there to be time there must be interaction
* for there to be interaction there must be multiplicity
* for there to be multiplicity there must be space.

In other words, and to modify the quotation from Bergson, time may indeed 'prevent everything from being given at once' (thought it's a wonderfully curious way of putting it!), but for there to be time, at least more than one thing must be given at once. For there to be time, there must be space.

Second, the school of French structuralism also worked with a conceptualisation of space which is thoroughly at variance with the one being proposed here, and again their influence can still be detected strongly at working the writings of their theoretical descendents – Ernest Laclau, for instance, and Michel de Certeau among others, including Michel Foucault. Again, as in the case of Bergson, the initial stimuli for the approach taken by the structuralists were ones with which this paper would have considerable sympathy, and once again they were really – centrally – concerned with time. Within anthropology in particular one impetus towards a 'structuralist' conceptualisation of the world derived from a wariness about the implications of the then hegemonic notions of temporal narrative. Too often, they argued, such narrative (temporal) ways of conceptualising the world led to classifications of levels of development which relegated the societies they were studying to the status of 'primitive', as only existing as forerunners of our own 'developed' status.

Structuralism argued for the coherence of such societies in their own right. In place of the dominance of temporal narrative they asserted the significance of internally coherent self-standing structures. So far so good.

The problem arose when this debate was translated (mis-translated, I would argue) into conceptualisations of (and dichotomies between) space and time. The structuralists were arguing against the dominance of temporality (in fact, a particular view of temporality). In their eagerness to do this, and in a leap of logic which may be understandable but which has absolutely no philosophical foundation, they equated their a-temporal structures with spatiality. The underlying assumption was that time and space were the opposite of each other, and that space was a lack of temporality. As with Bergson, then, the structuralists, set time and space in opposition to each other (Bergson supporting time, the structuralists space) and as with Bergson the spatial was understood as the sphere of stasis and of fixity.

There was no need, even in the structuralists' project, for this to have happened. For the structures which they proposed, thought they may have been lacking in temporality, were in no sense spatial. They were simply atemporal. They only came to be called spatial because of an over-easy assumption that a lack of time must mean one is dealing with space.

This vision of spatiality as stasis, moreover, was reinforced by their conceptualisation of the structures themselves. For these they imagined a totally interlocking system of relations. 'Space', then, was understood not just as a synchrony but as a closed synchrony, and opposed to a diachrony. Certainly, then, this notion of spatiality accords with this paper's first proposition: that space is a product of interrelations. But it is in complete contradiction to the third proposition: that space is always in a process of becoming; that it is never a closed system. It was this stasis of their structures and to the unbridgeable oppositions between such pairs as 'langue' and 'parole'. And thus it is that Certeau writes:

...spatialisation of scientific discourse...scientific writing ceaselessly reduces time, that fugitive element, to the normality of an observable and readable system.

Doreen Massey

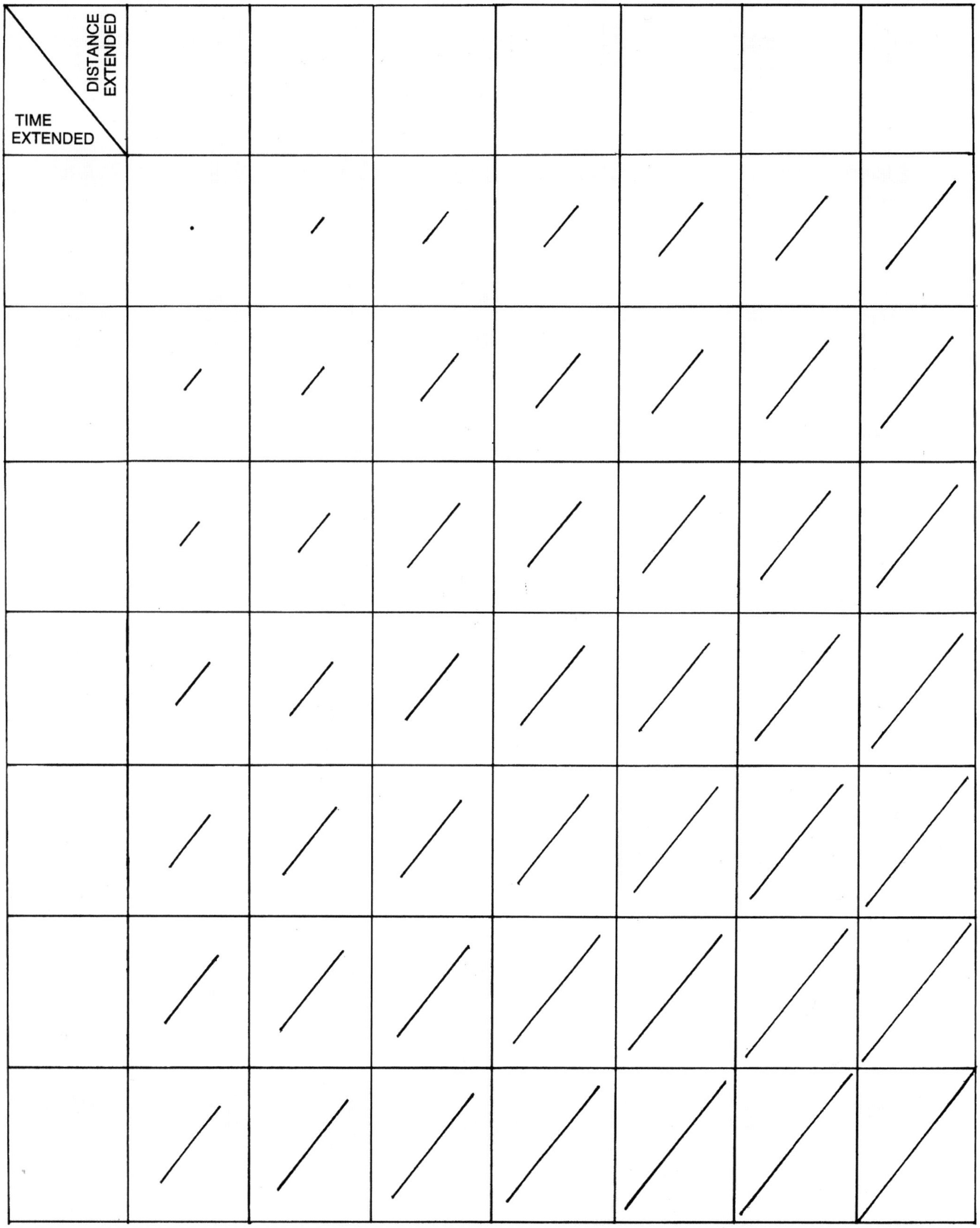

DISTANCE EXTENDED / TIME EXTENDED							

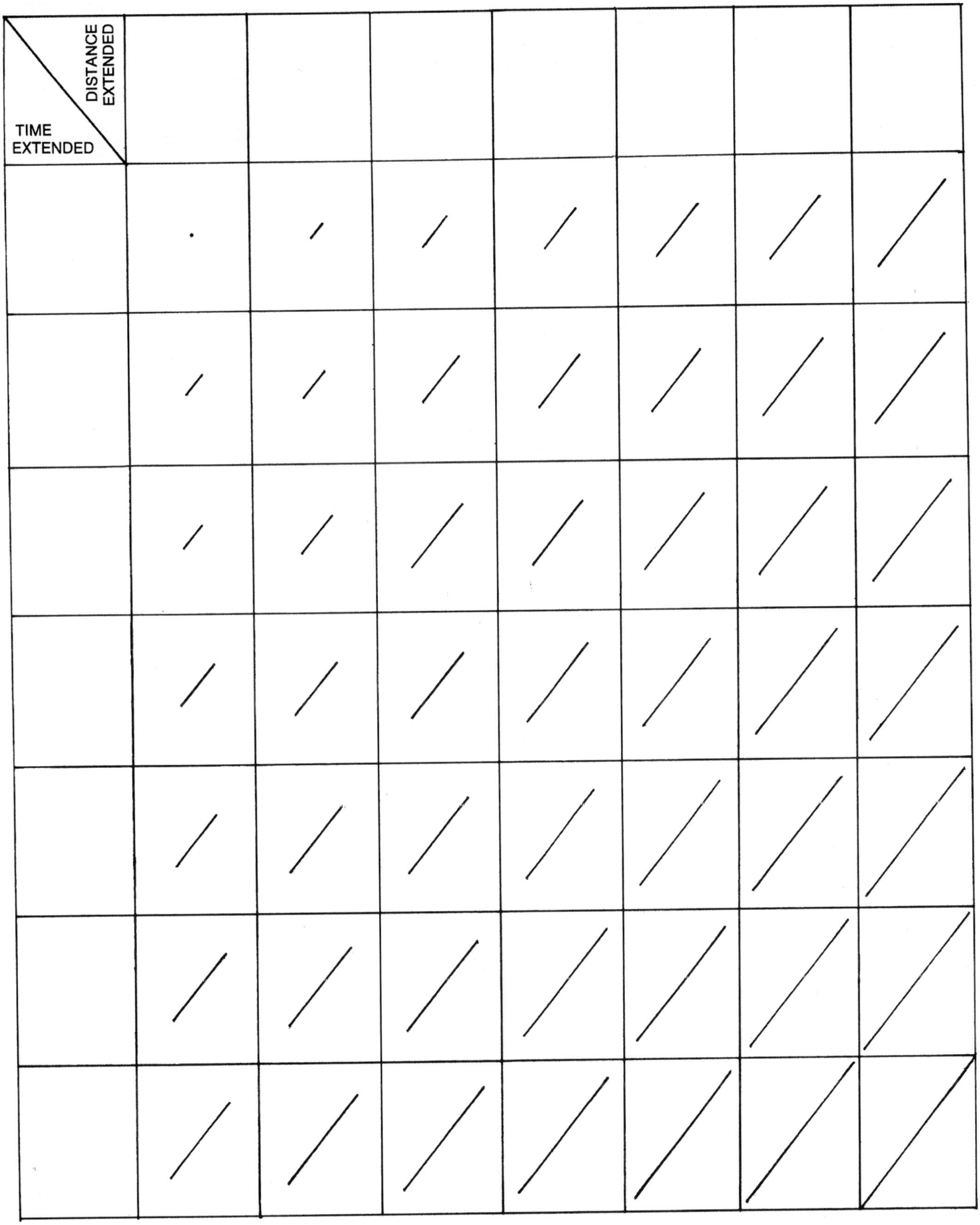

DISTANCE EXTENDED

TIME EXTENDED

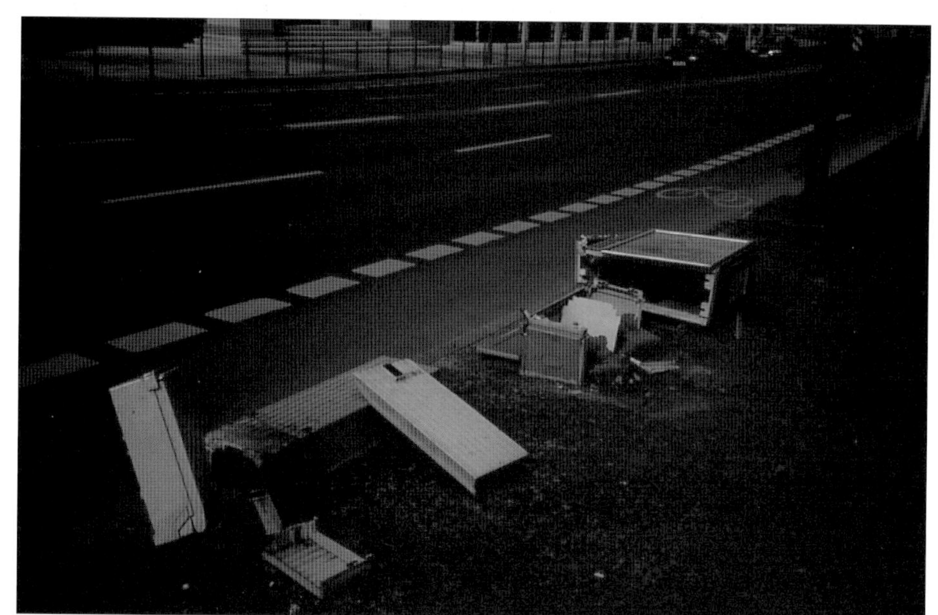

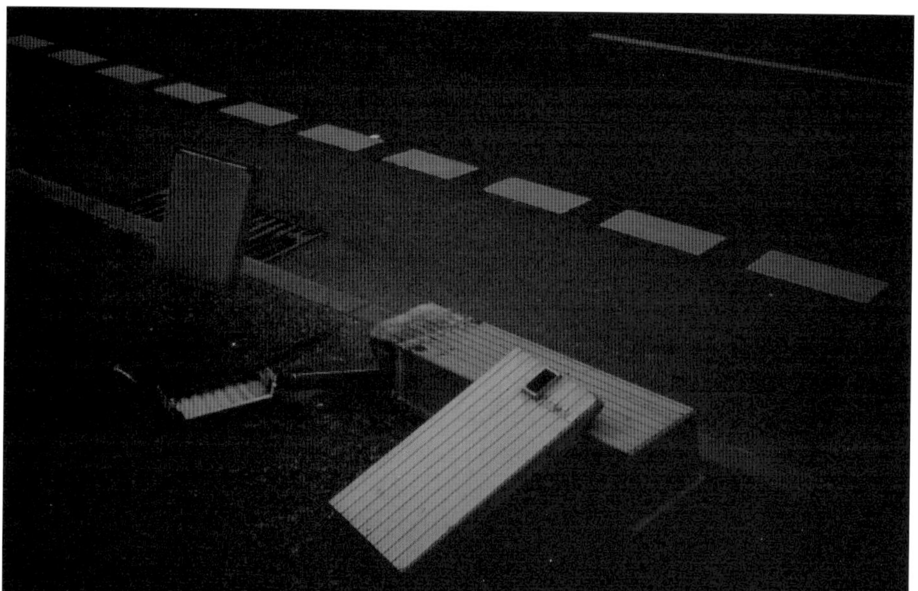

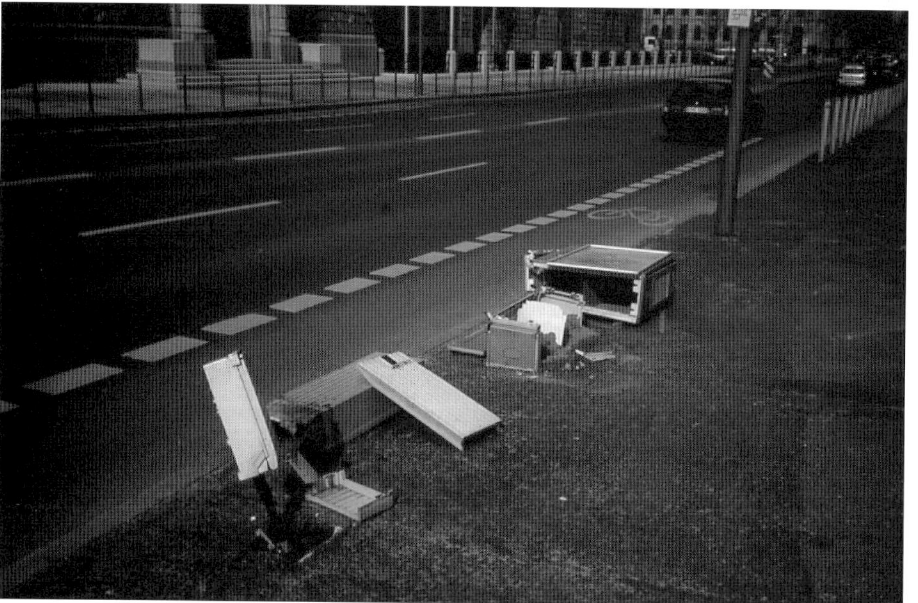

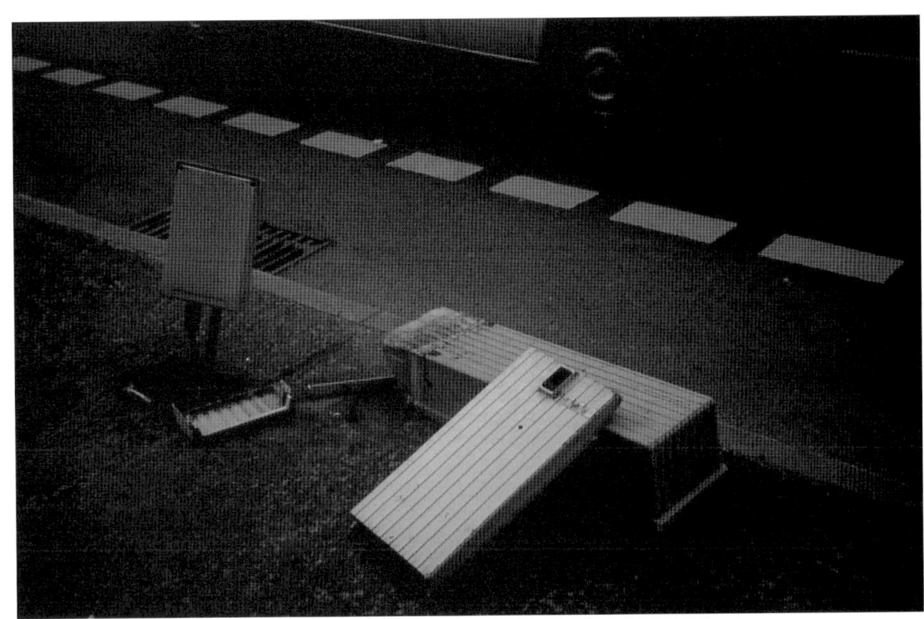

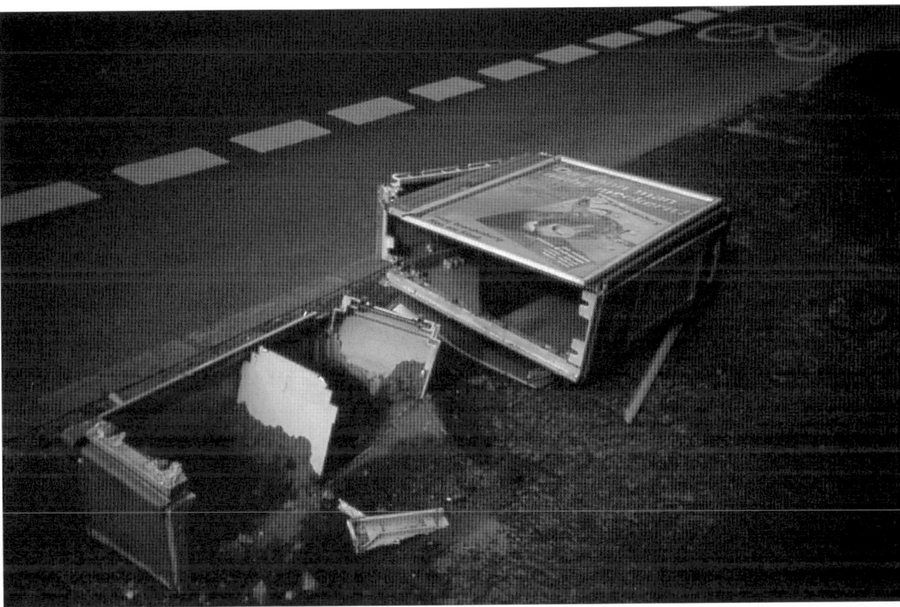

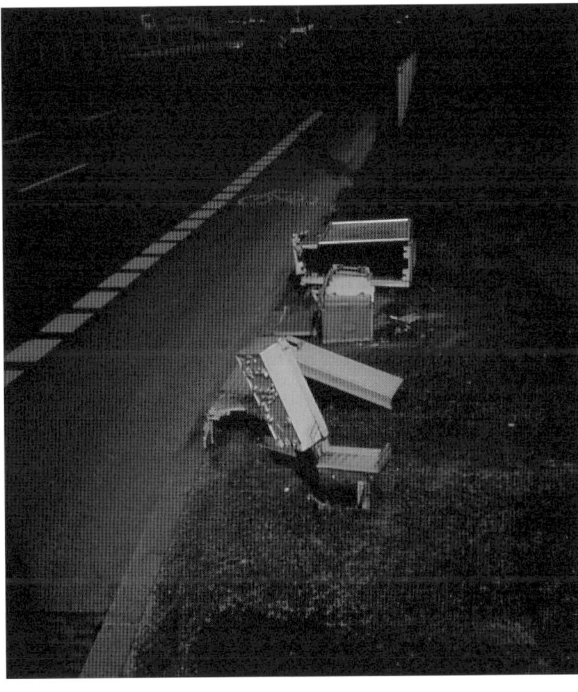

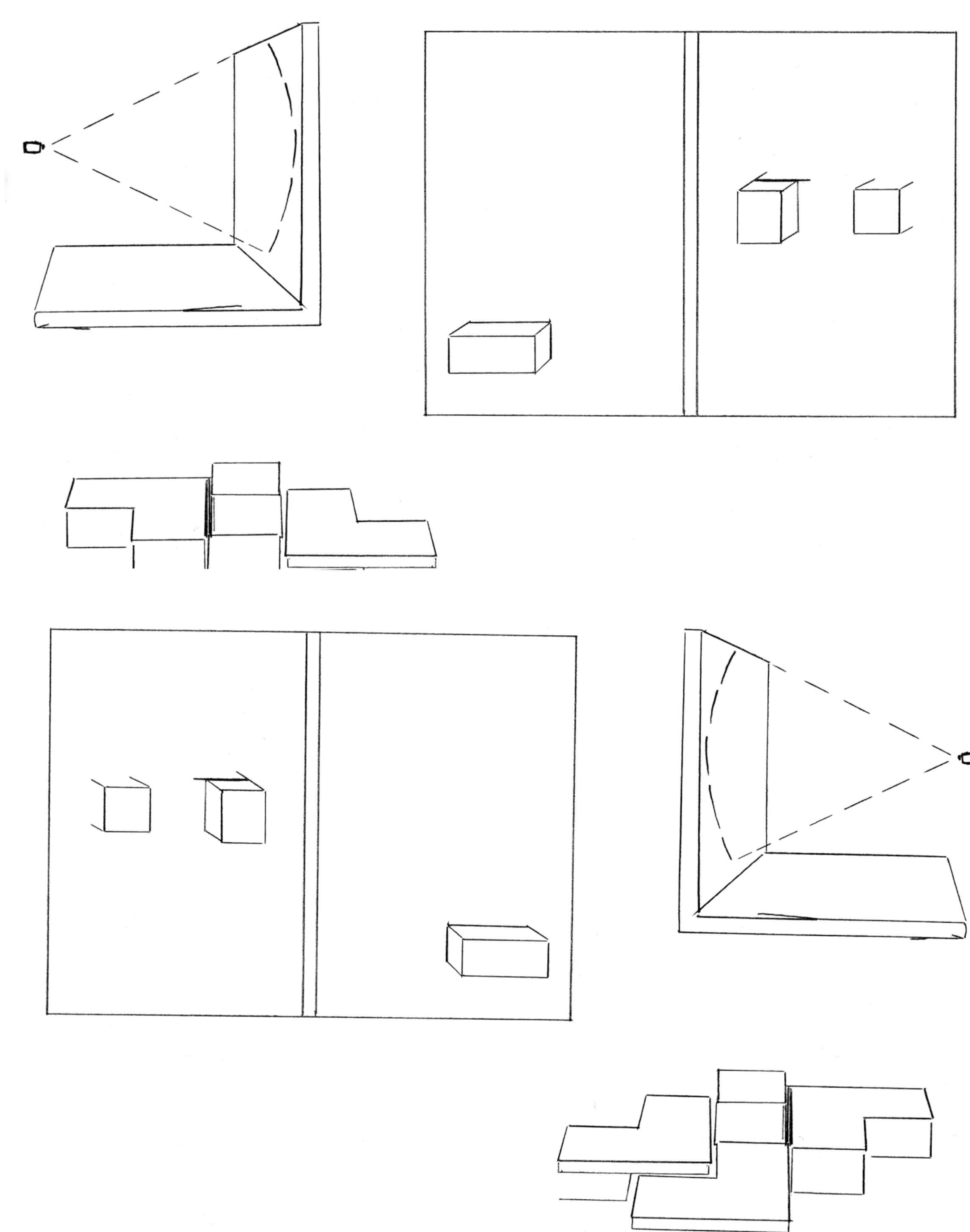

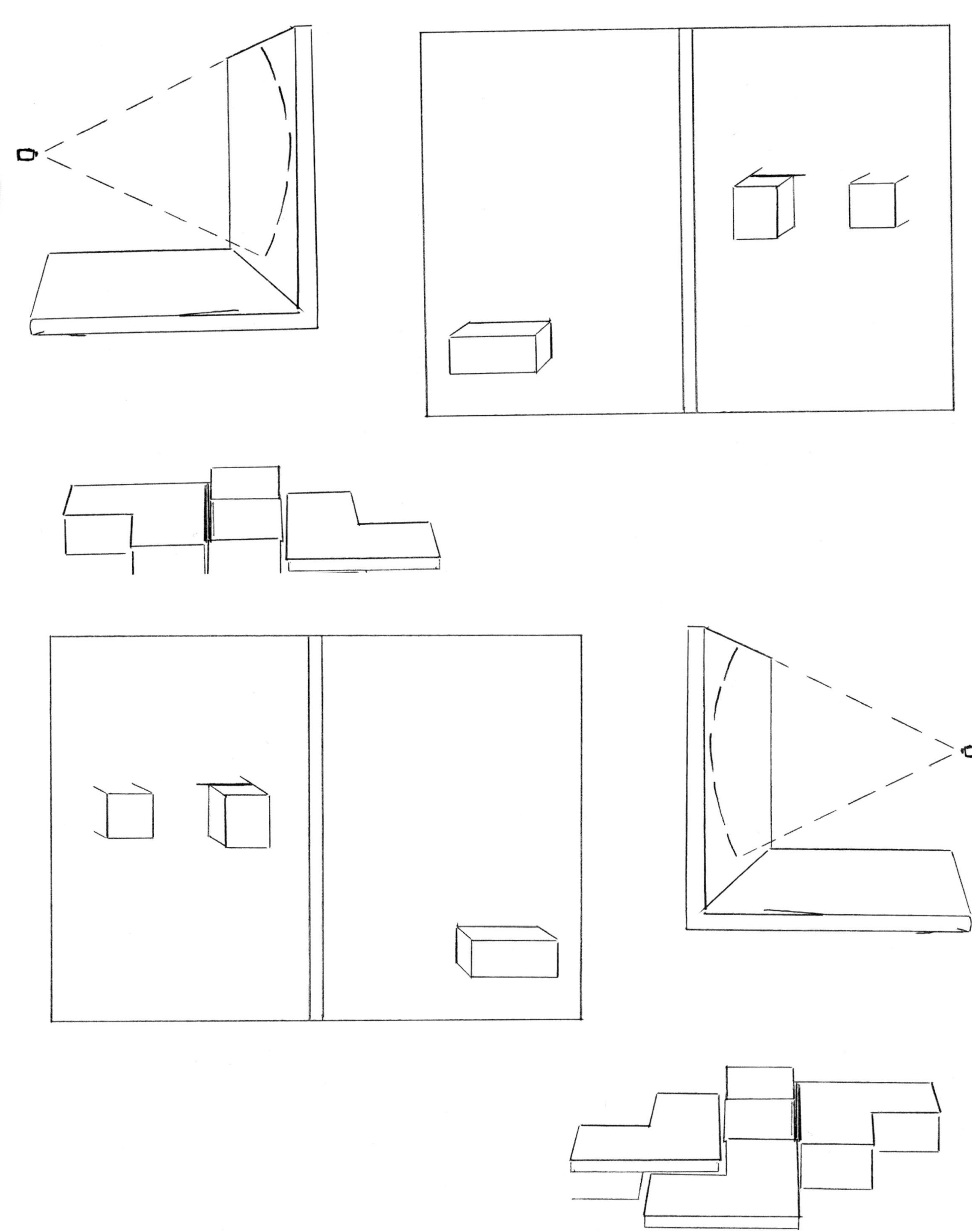

```
<meta http-equiv="content-type" content="text/html;charset=utf-8"/>
<meta http-equiv="Content-Style-Type" content=""/>
</head>

</span></font></div>
<div align="left"><font face="Arial" size="2"><span style="font-size: 10pt"><br />
</span></font></div>
<div align="left"><font face="Arial" black="#00007f" size="2"><span  style="font-
size:10pt"><b><u></u></b></span></font></div>
<div align="left"><font face="Arial" size="2"><span style="font-size: 10pt">font= span style
</span></ font></div>
10pt">Buzari</span></font></div>
<div align="left"><font face="Arial" size="2"><span style="font-size: 10pt"><br />
</span></font></div>
<div align="left"></div>
</html>
```

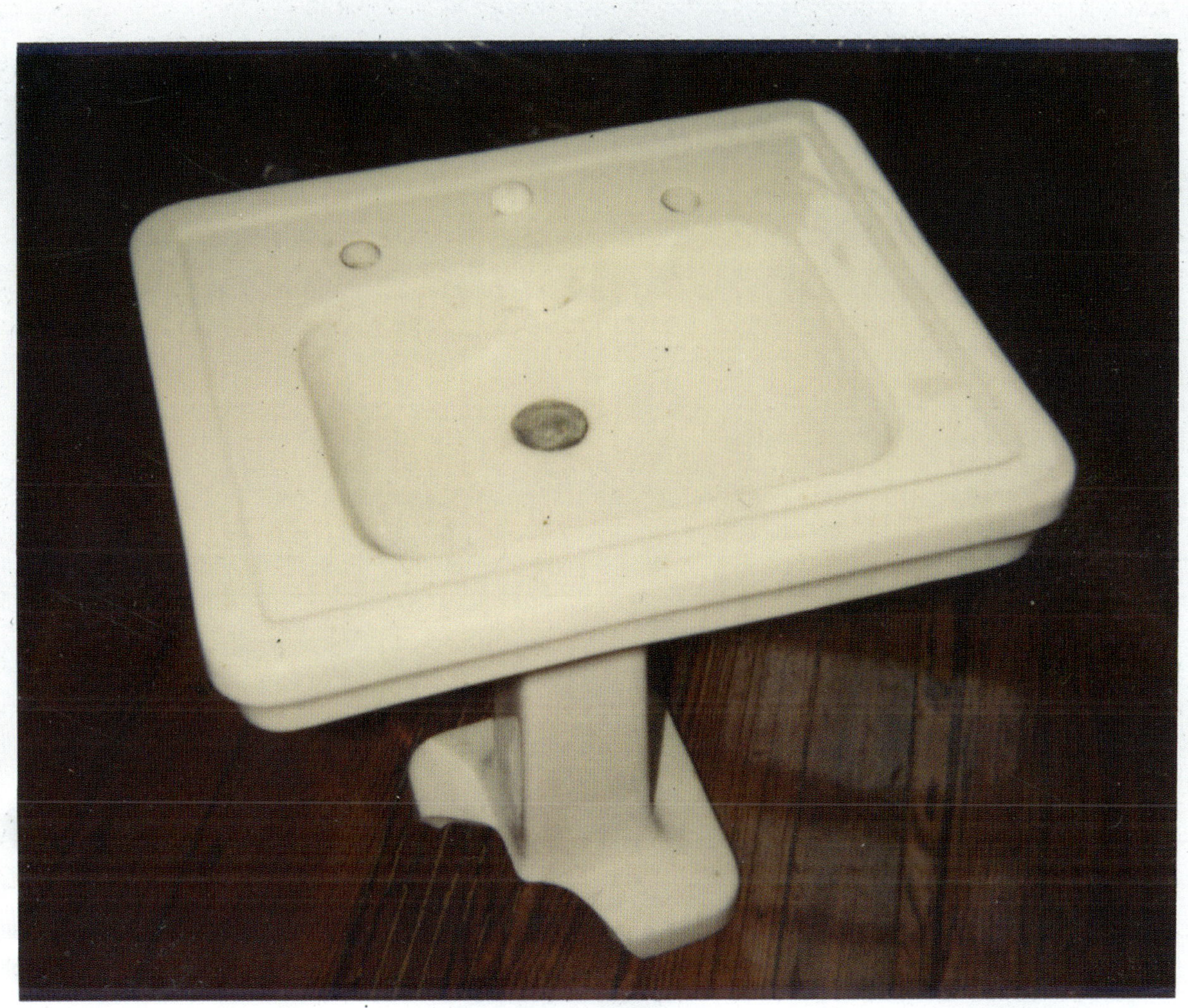

Scale Model of lavatory — Trenton

Maddock — 1 of 3

Phonoglutamate

Philip K Dick said, "If you find this world bad, you should try some of the other ones". Even science fiction authors seem to have abandoned the task of describing the near future. With his novels Snow Crash and Diamond Age, for example, Neil Stephenson became a science fiction darling, writing for Wired Magazine, earning awards and comparisons to cyberpunk giants such as Bruce Sterling and William Gibson. But in his two last two books, first in Cryptonomicon, he depicts the 20th century from World War II code breaking and disinformation to the latest issues of internet data privacy, and more recently in Quicksilver he goes through the 17th century to detail events that threw the entire world upside-down. He is going backwards. Bruce Sterling's last book is an essay entitled Tomorrow Now and William Gibson published Pattern Recognition which takes place in our upgraded present. Interesting. And yesterday I bought the latest Beach Boy album with great pleasure and impatience.

People have been concerned with finding their place in a physical, political or social space for a long time. For example, all of Velasquez's paintings are concerned with spatial problems. Space was like glue. Our problems are different now. They date back to 1972, the year the last few radical architecture groups disappeared and Spielberg, Lukas, Scorsese and Coppola took over Hollywood. Some could precisely date it at 3:32 pm on July 15, 1972 when the Pruit-Igo housing development was blasted in St Louis, Missouri. It had been a prize-winning example of the clean-lined, boxy, international style of architecture and what architects called a "machine for living". By 1972 it was considered a failure. People hated it and the city declared it uninhabitable. The same year Robert Venturi declared that most people's ideas were closer to Disneyland or Las Vegas than to a modern glass-box apartment.

From that point on, our lives have been based on a time protocol. We have a need to register ourselves in time. For this, as well as for the New Wave, Serge Beauvialat invented the "Time Code".

We need tools to edit our lives. Looking becomes a movement into the dimensions of the pictogram, a fall through the impossible topology of n dimensions.

Yes, it's hard to deal with the present, just think of Andy Warhol. He made portraits with movie cameras, filming people in real time without editing - a person sleeping, a person in a moment of glory. Some might say that it's still discomforting to watch his films today. Perhaps because the subjects are looking directly at us, perhaps it's because we know they are now dead, or maybe it's just because the images are cruel and unforgiving. Andy Warhol was the first visual artist to index human representation using a time frame. This was no post-modern gesture, like installing Greek columns in a social housing estate. In 13 Beautiful Girls, thirteen top models stared at the camera, motionless and without blinking so that they would resemble fixed images. But it's very difficult to resemble an image; we've all tried, especially as children. But now, as adults, we know that by not blinking we end up crying.

It's hard to think about the present because the past always glows.

In the good old days before cappuccino and sushi and ruccola went global. Well before red peppers spiced up our salads. Before adventure became a sport, and nature became a spot. In the good old days the Paris Metro smelled like cigarettes and lofts were reserved for only the New-York elite. Before seat belts beeped when they weren't fastened and spies really did come from the cold. Before cell phone conversations were banned on trains. Before googling became an aspect of human behavior. In the good old days when every second person was not a hero and every third was not a victim and every fourth was not stressed. Before we had an identity on line. Before toll-free numbers were delocalized and sent to Africa or India. Before the idea of a preemptive war existed. Before we thought there would never be any billionaires in Moscow. Before beach volleyball and snowboarding became Olympic sports. Before fusion cooking and before liquid nitrogen was used to make minute ice cream. Before you could get an espresso in Hamburg or Milwaukee. When Thai food was exotic and cholesterol a curious word used only for Scrabble games. In the good old days when people walked on the moon and snow covered London for weeks during Christmas time. No, it's too far away, I don't remember all that. It never happened.

A time when things were not weird, but strange, and then they were really strange, a David Lynch kind of strangeness. In those disconnected days before Blackberries and SPVs. Before voicemail became the interlocutors in our lives. Before Godlum appeared on the screen. What a great actor. Before the Euro and before a wall was erected in Israel. Before democracy and free market became the only alternative. When New Zealand was not yet known as the set of The Lord of The Rings. Before people started using "like" to make similes about anything and everything. Before Shrek appeared on screen and everyone loved him because like us, he doesn't understand any metaphors. When you could smoke in bars in New York and Los Angeles. Before the Bush Dynasty. When Schwarzenegger was the Terminator and not a governor. Before IPods, EBay, Viagra and spell-check. Before Western architects were lining up to build towers in China. Before people start ordering salads at McDonald's. Before music became our soundtrack. Before clothing became a costume. Before we start looking at the world as a standing stock of material. Before the word "tree" did not mean "wood".

Pay attention. Take notes.

Philippe Pareno

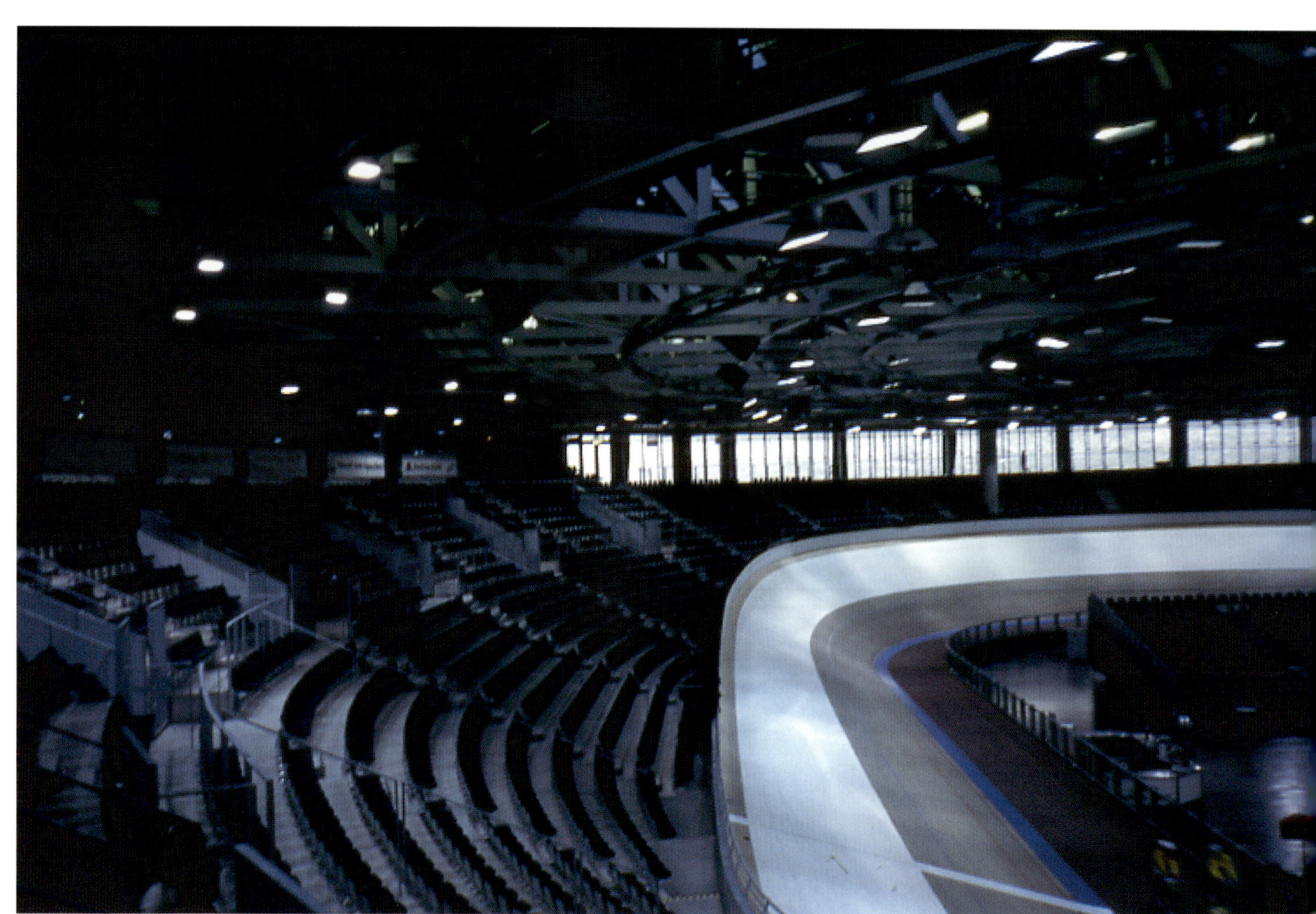

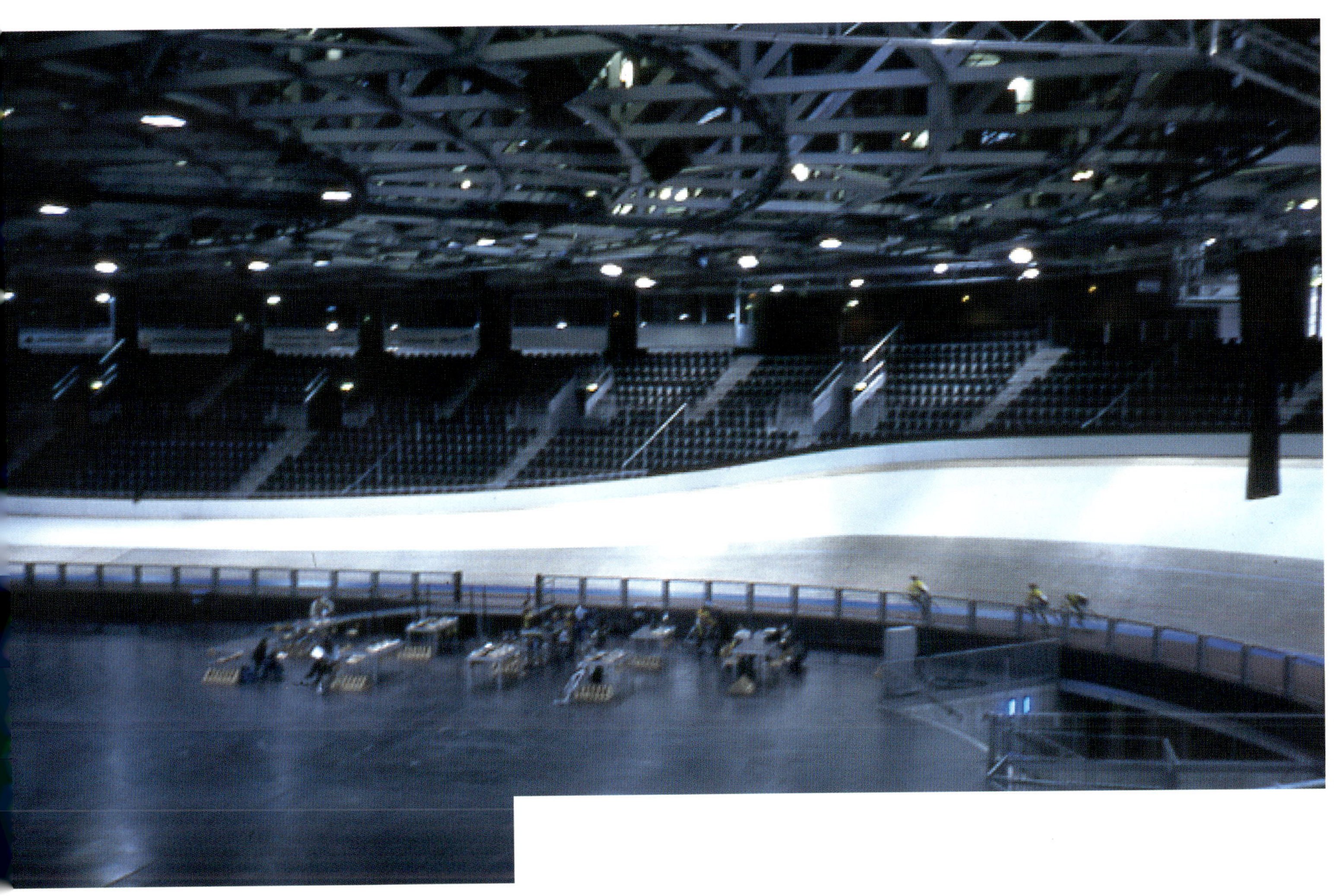

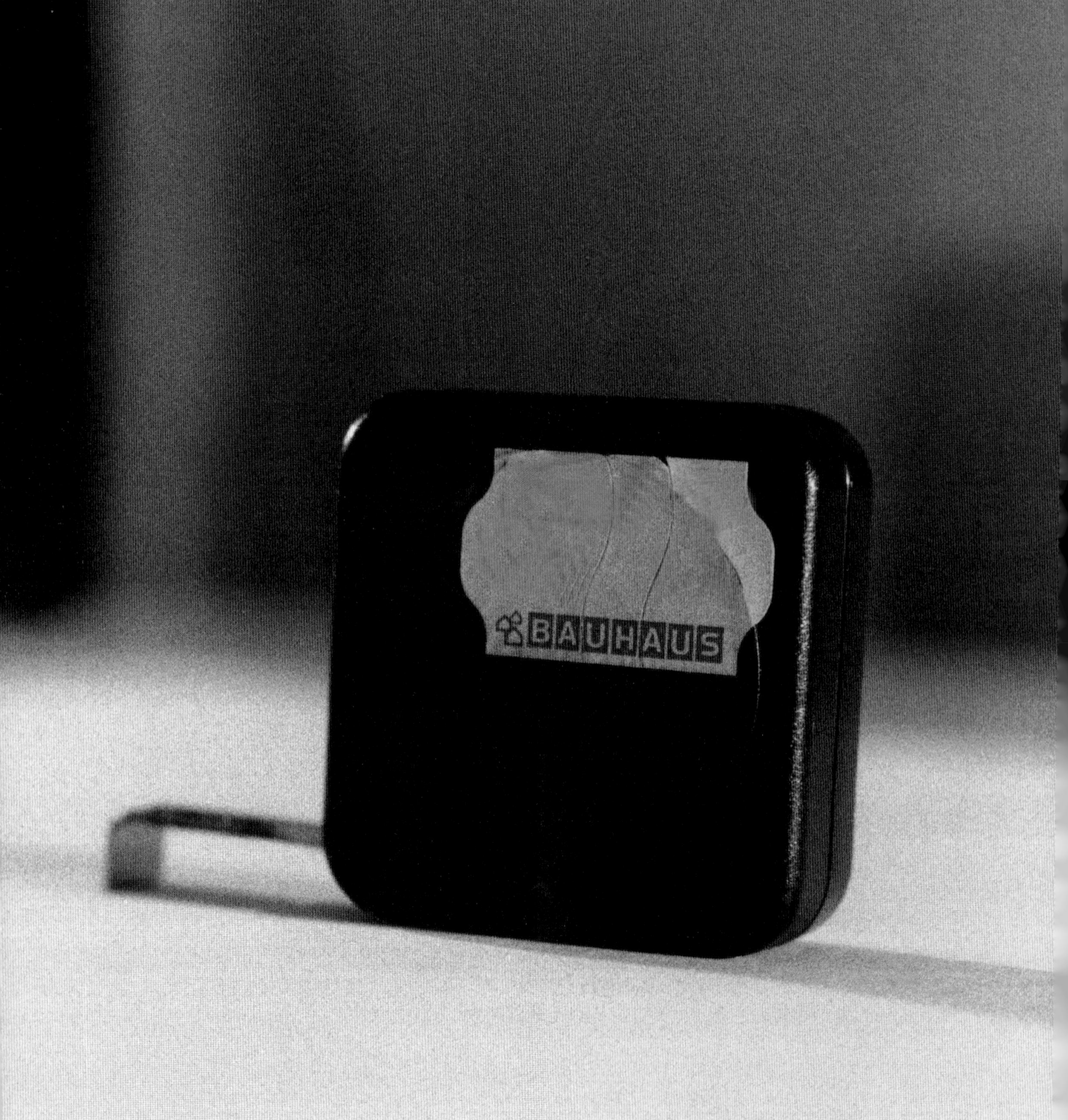
BAUHAUS

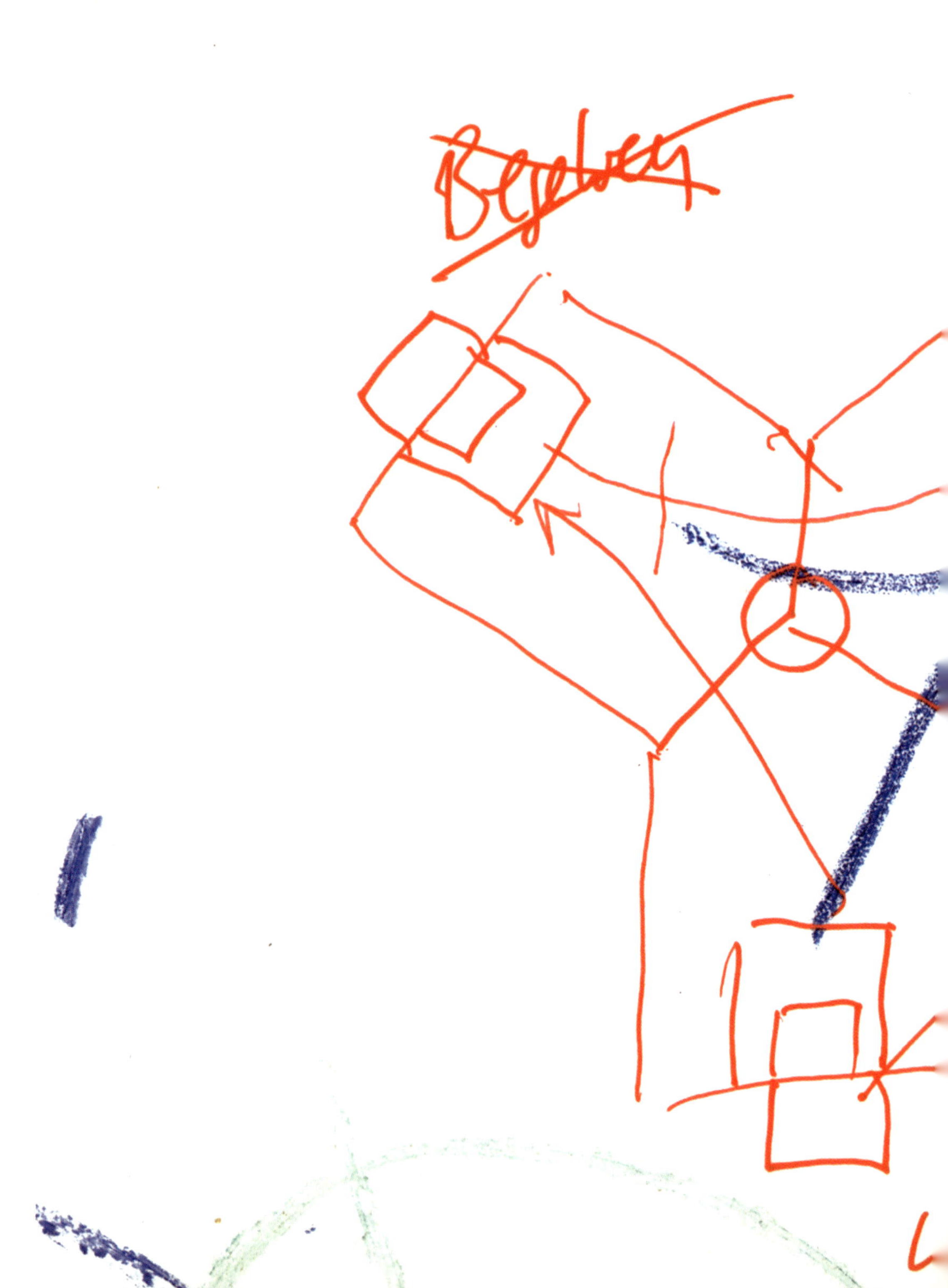

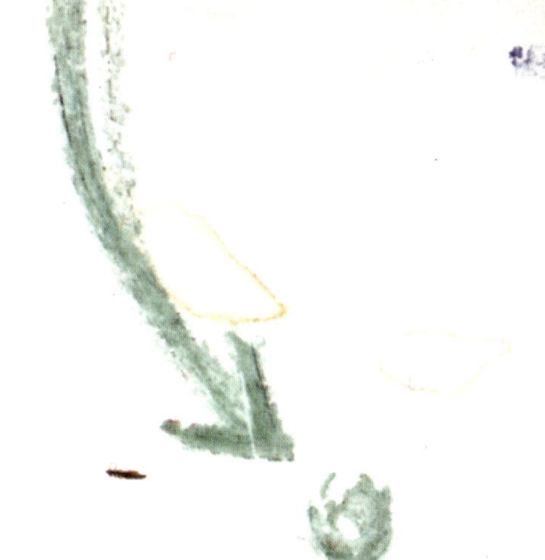

Politik

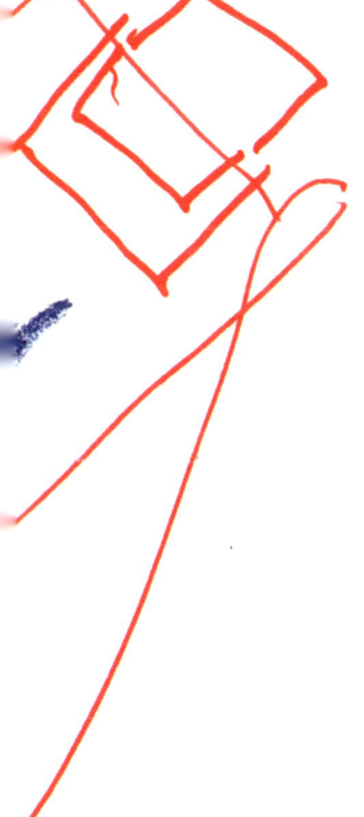

noh

Hans Ulrich Obrist
So, yeah, Rainbows in Curved Air, the title.

Pash Buzari
Yes, Rainbows in Curved Air is the title of the Publication. It has a music reference and it is a variation with a kind of more radical twist on a theme of Terry Riley A Rainbow in Curved Air.

HUO
I know him, I interviewed him, actually.

PB
Okay, how was it?

HUO
Very good, it's on going.
... is his work also kind of like a trigger.

PB
... in a way... I like this kind of affinity to ...this mantra type of repetition where you kind of enter into something different after a while. Like being in this steady loop and then suddenly you're in this kind of „new space" – You constantly repeat something, like playing a favorite song on and on, you constantly repeat it and then somehow the previous idea of it get's lost...

HUO
...Repetition, no?

PB
Well, okay, may be repetition of the repetition –
I am more or less taking it as a kind of surface, starting from these kind of surfaces, and basically adding them up. Similar to these Videoclips from the 70's and 80's, where they were using this visual feedback effect and you would see the same image infinitely multiplied ... a loop of loops.

HUO
Can you tell me about the structure of the book? Because it basically raises an identity related to other pieces but at the same time it's an artist book, it's a catalogue. Can you tell me a little bit about the status about the publication?

PB
Rainbows in Curved Air should work more like a loose and fragmented material collection of images and texts. Related to the idea of collapsing and redundant spaces which has been a red line in my Biennale piece. About how architecture moves into areas of dysfunction, specially within the context of social utopias where a lot of architecture has been built, with a specific purpose... and then suddenly along the line of collapsing ideologies, constructions, buildings, monuments etc. „collapse" as well. So this is like a...

HUO
A failed utopia?

PB
A failed utopia, yeah, well - i am not even sure if the notion „utopia" is really that relevant ... the idea of failure is definitely not so important here or at least it could be neclected – i am more interested into „extension".. you remember my contribution for the Utopia Station Poster Series, the „Bauhaus" Photograph.. One idea there was that the historical Bauhaus, with it's aim to influence societies for example by providing „high quality" design for a mass public arrives at an interesting level, when it somehow virtually converts into a contemporary toolshop, which 50 years later it seem to appropriate the name.

Even though i don't know if this was intentional, because „Bauhaus" could as well be used as a common notion, like „built a house"... but in any case it becomes this place, where everyone can actually access the means of production for their own „space" – so in a way this is an extension of the former idea, a kind of „ extended utopia" perhaps... the idea of self designed homes today...

Excerpt from an Interview by Hans Ulrich Obrist

TIME EXTENDED / DISTANCE EXTENDED							

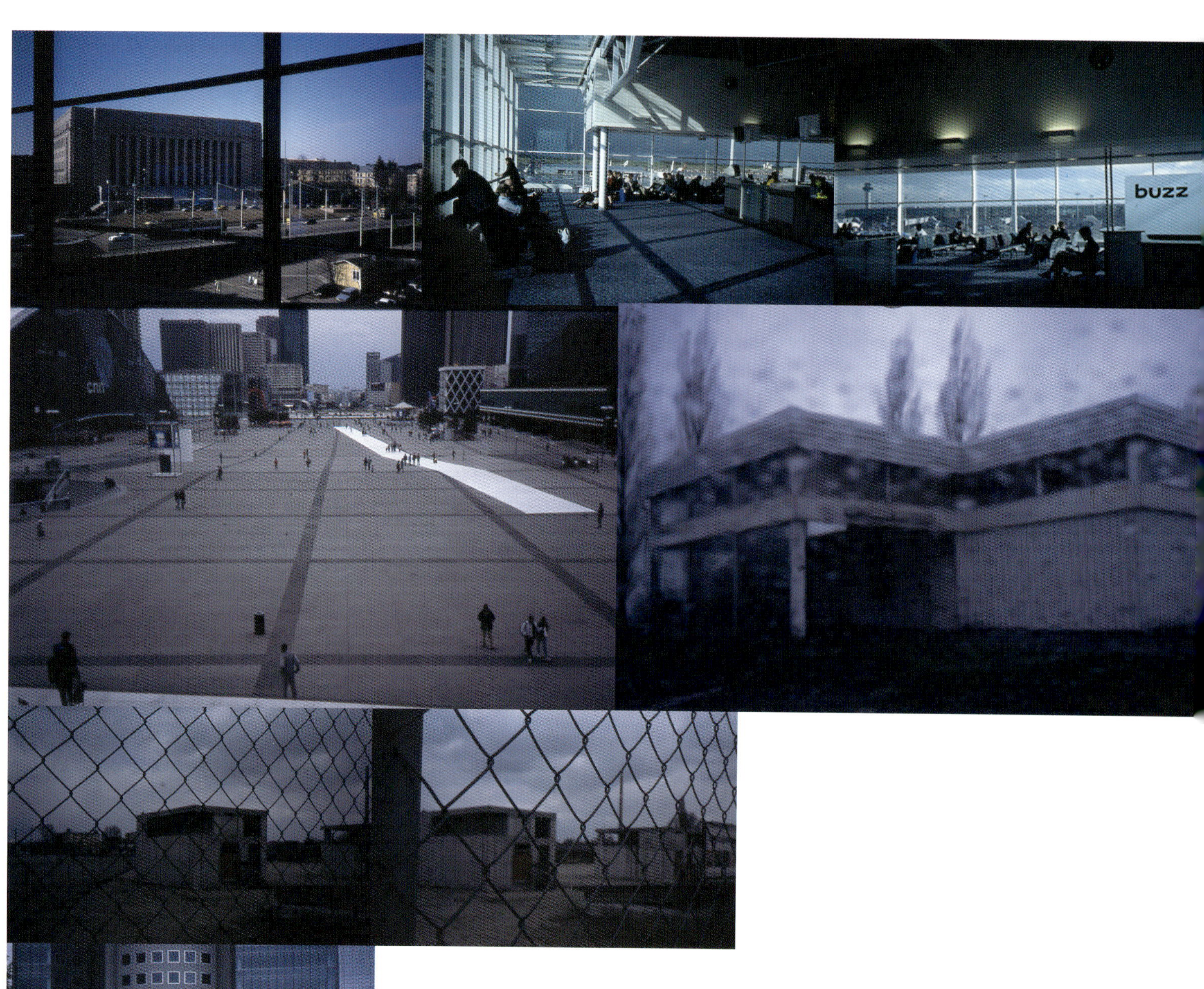
buzz

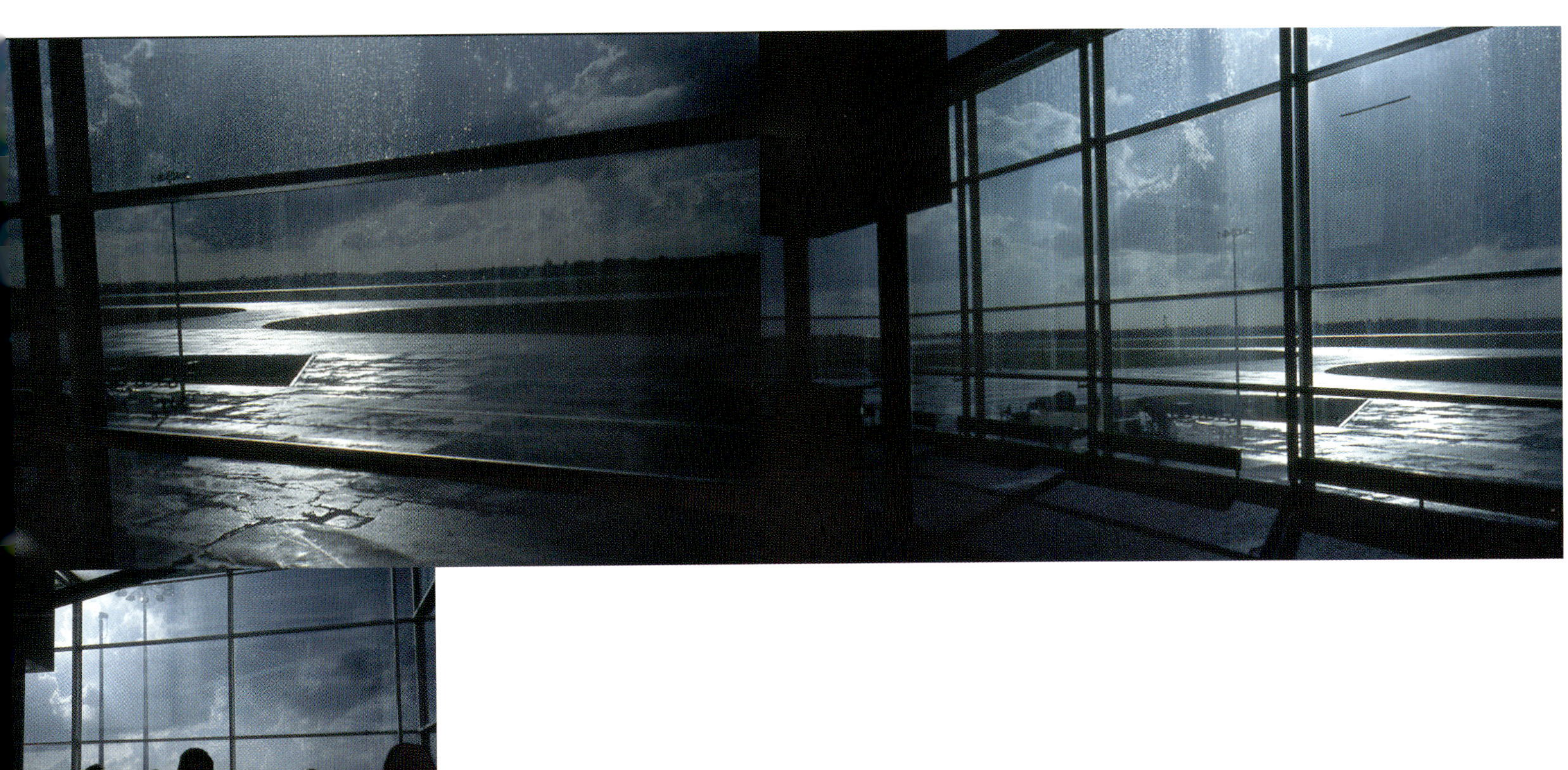

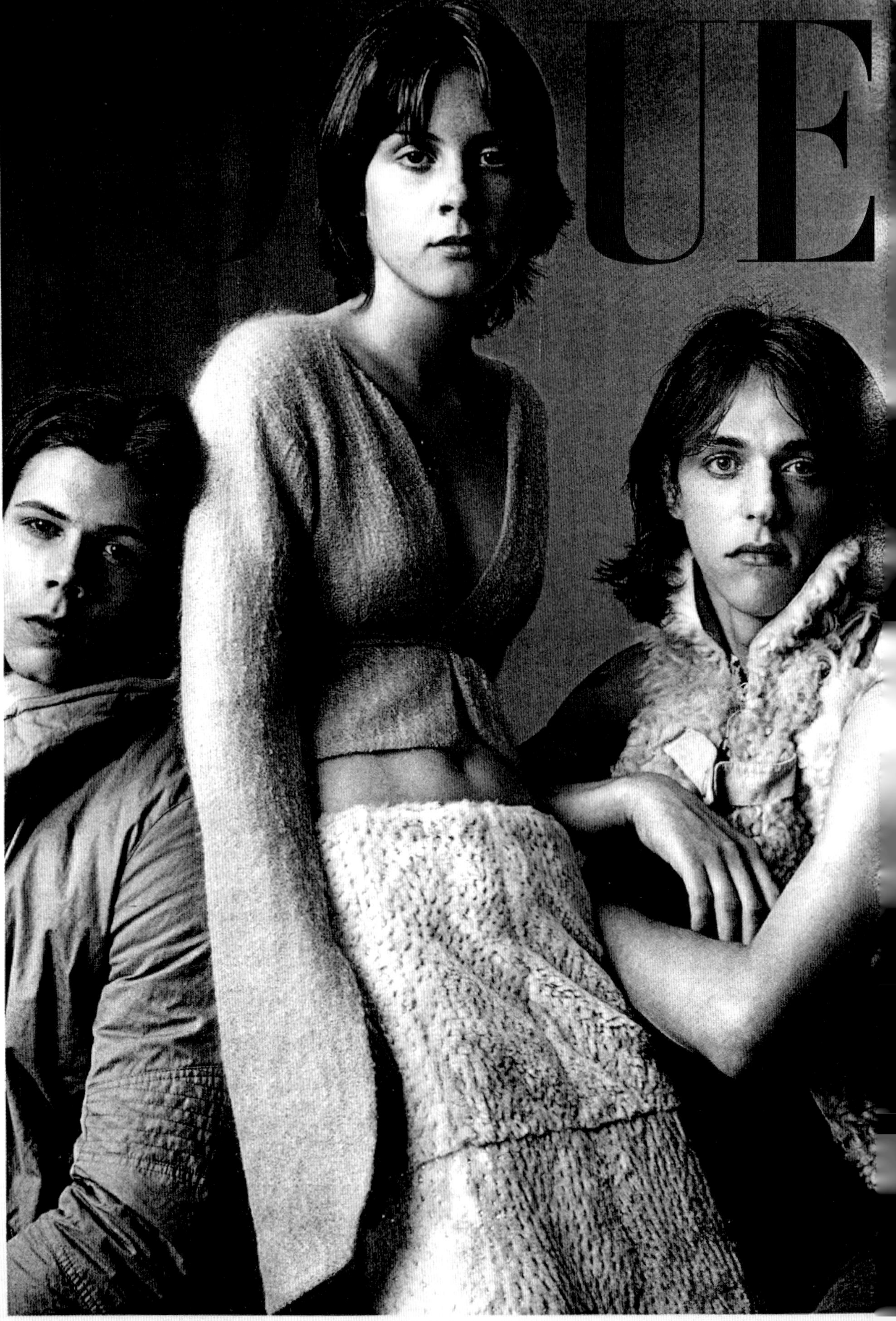
UE

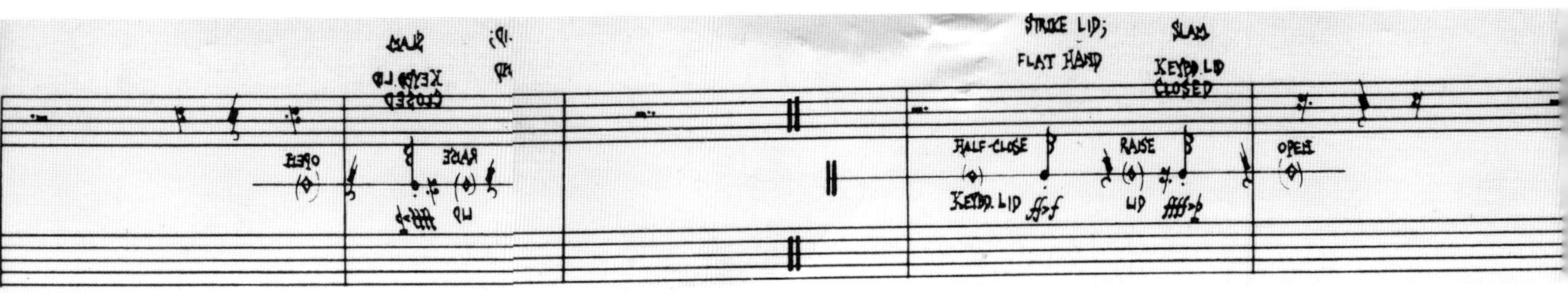

STRIKE LID;
FLAT HAND
SLAM
KEYBD. LID
CLOSED
HALF-CLOSE
KEYBD. LID
RAISE
LID
OPEN

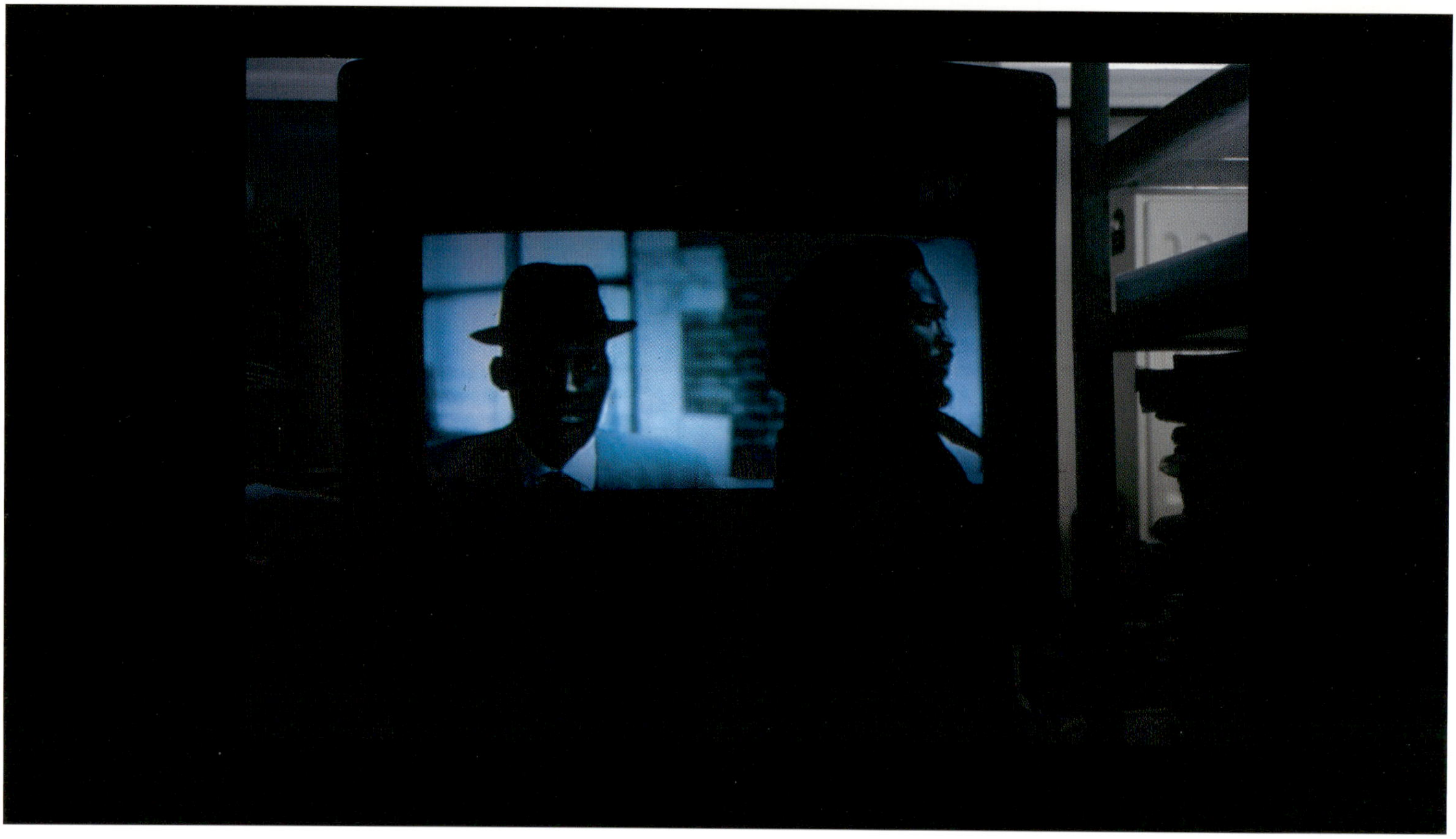

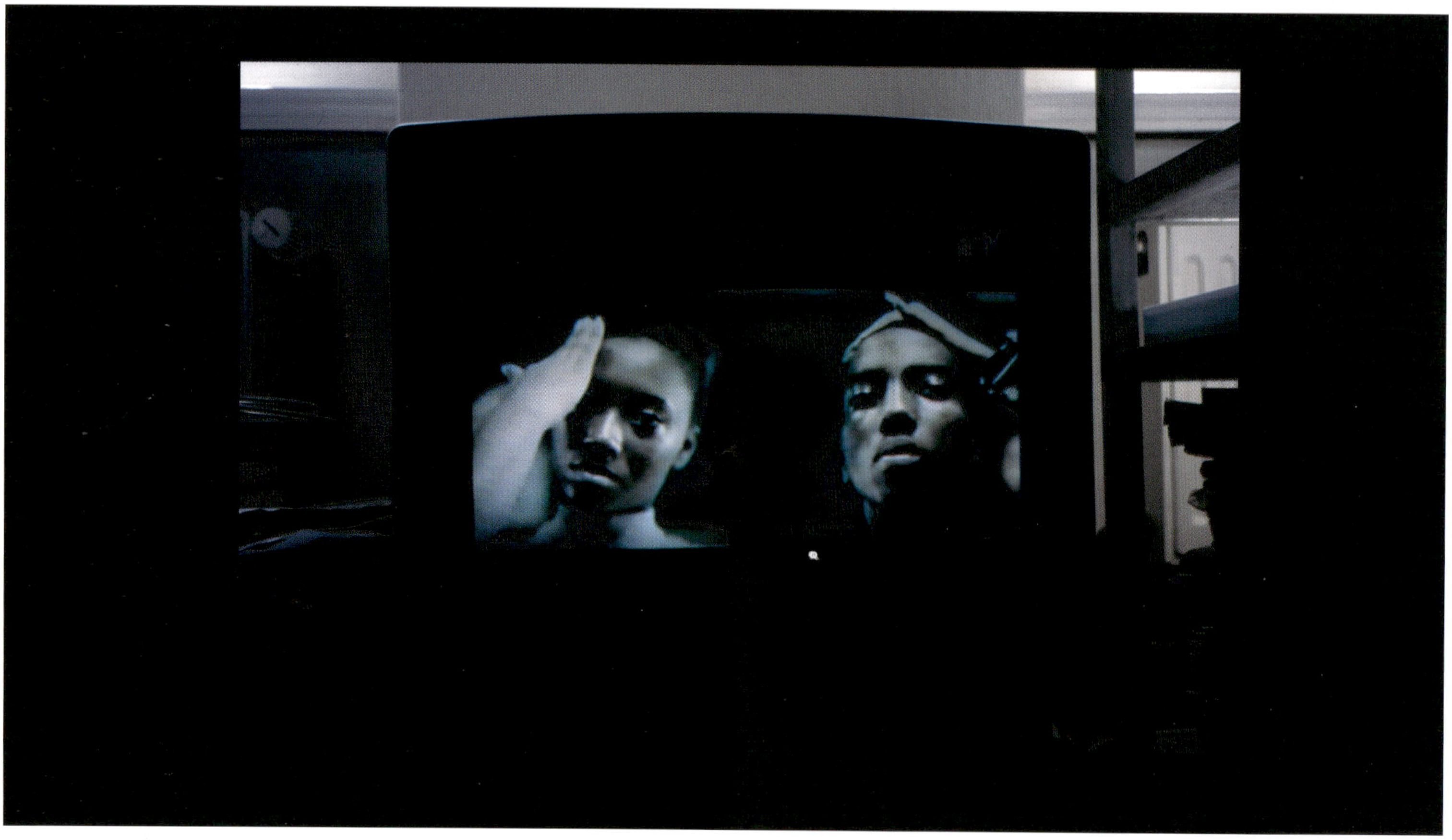

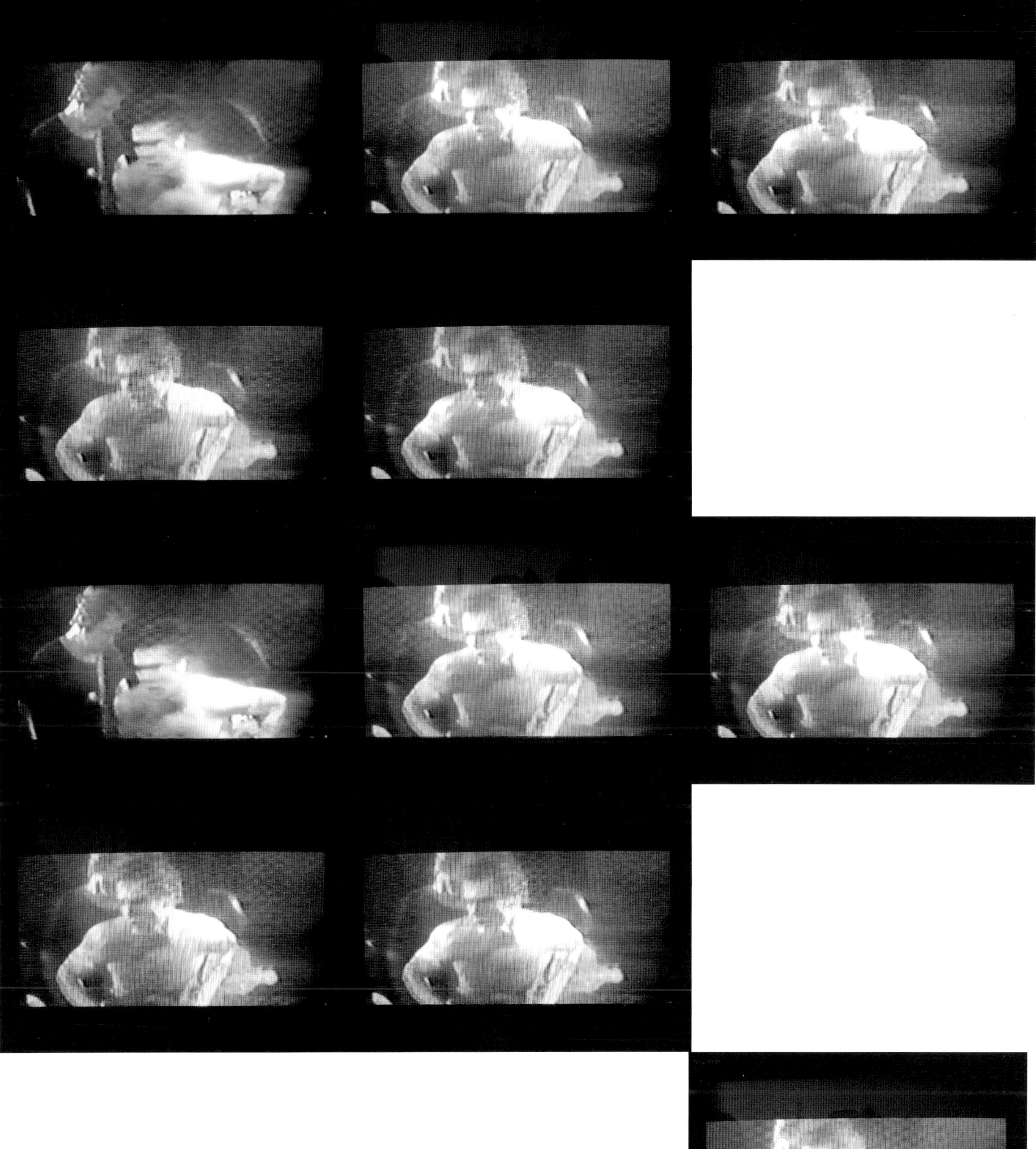

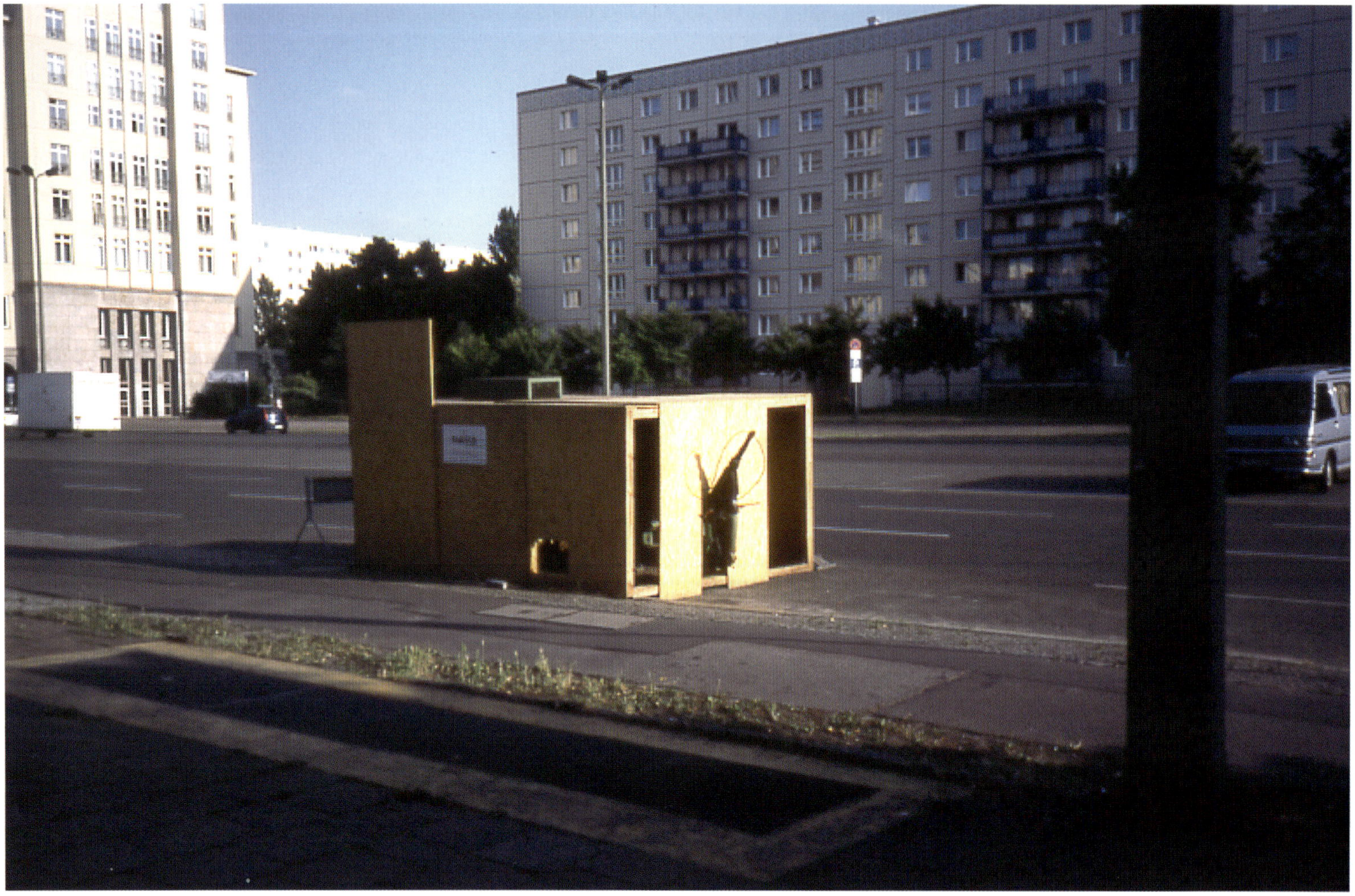

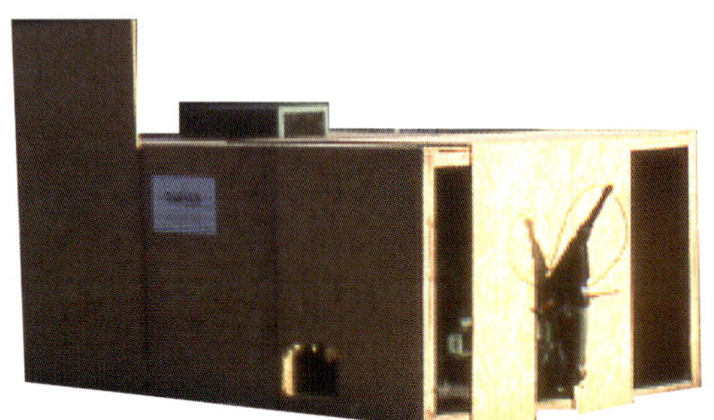

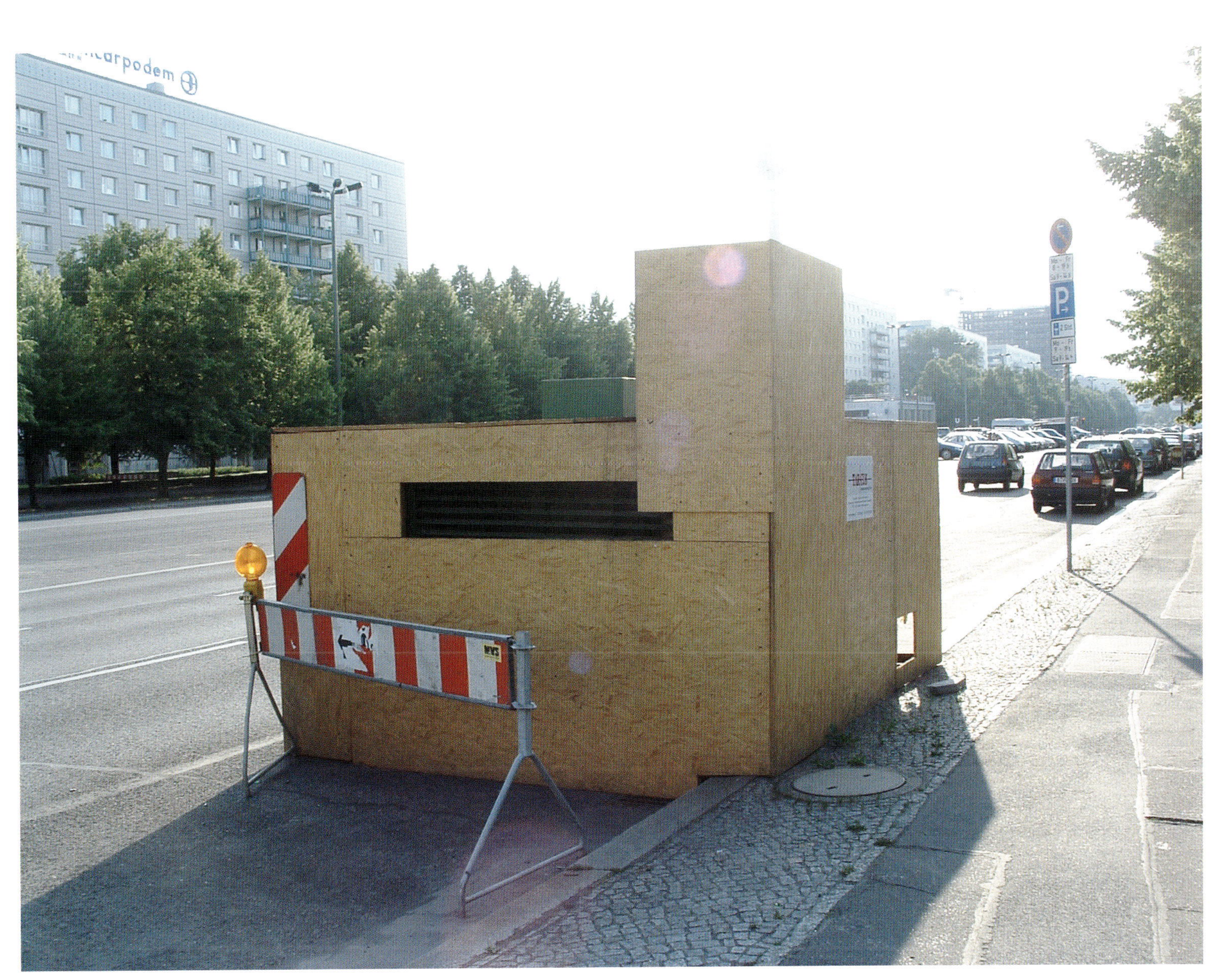

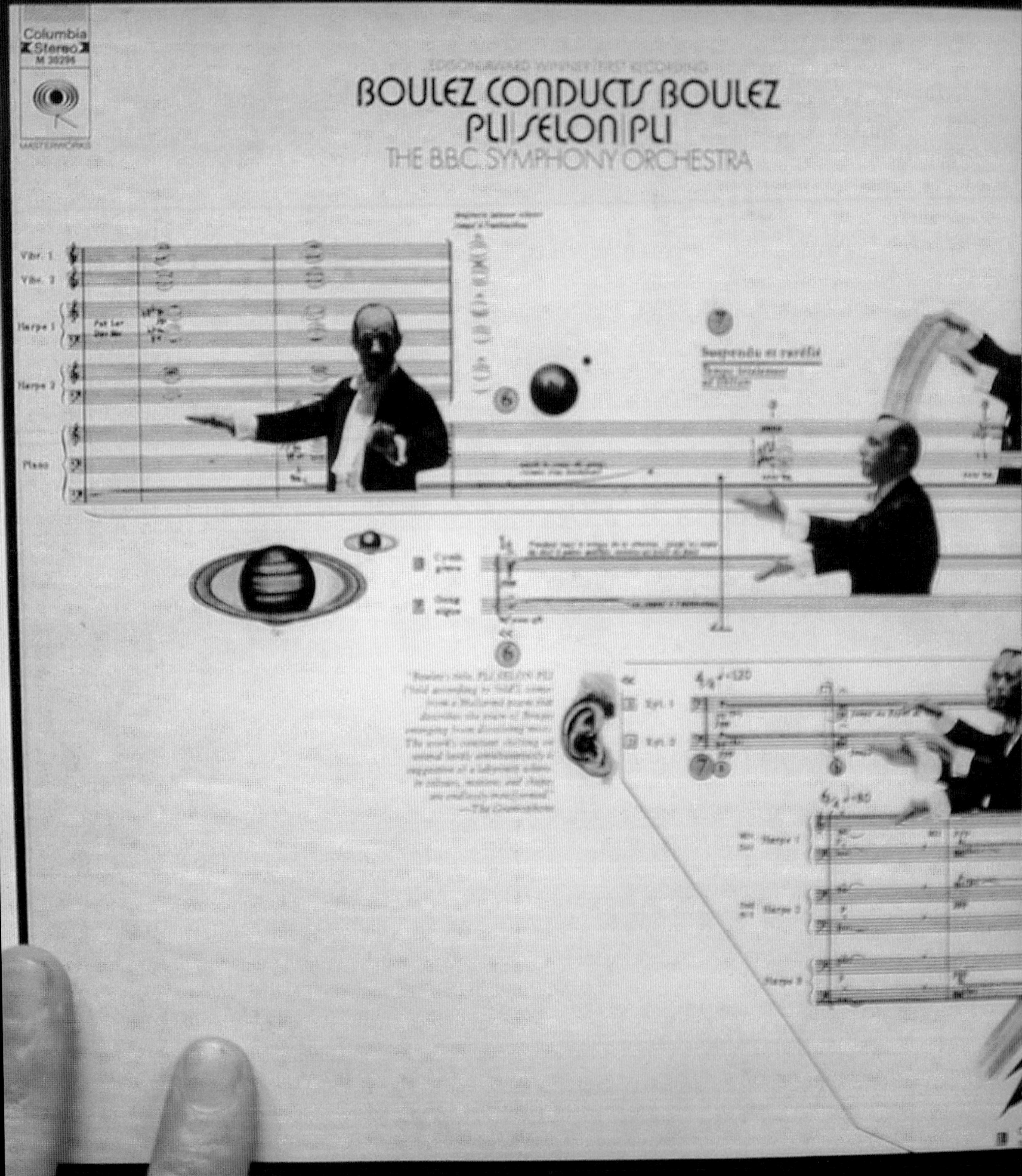

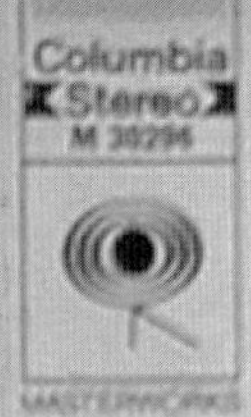

EDISON AWARD WINNER / FIRST RECORDING

BOULEZ CONDUCTS BOULEZ
PLI SELON PLI
THE B.B.C. SYMPHONY ORCHESTRA

This and That...

We have to try to investigate the relationship and non-relationship between "construction" and "destruction" in art and architecture and beyond in a more general and, at the same time, specific way.
Assuming construction/destruction were inherent in any immaterial and environmental process which runs through societies, indistinctly and massively, this would be a disaster of overwhelming power. The more this force becomes aesthetical and social, the more it would acquire from us an intellectual and political desire response. And if reconstruction/redestruction is already spread out in a universalized way, it will, as we speak, occupy the whole of society and permeate all of it's particles. I believe that construction/destruction is no longer merely ideological: rather it is functional and inate. We have to ask ourselves: how can it be reconstructed/redestroyed?
It is the reconstruction/redestruction that we feel somehow bearing down on us; our thoughts and dreams are implicated in it. In this dizzy light, we might think that "constructionalisms" of any sphere ought to be equivalent to "destructionalisms". It would, however, be crazy to draw such a conclusion, and if construction was expressed through the absence of destruction, it would indeed have a feel of madness about it.
But, what does construction/destruction imply then?
Reconstruction/redestruction is a force - not only in the fields of art and architechture - which is beautiful, powerful and unclear, and this is what we should be exploring.

Pash Buzari

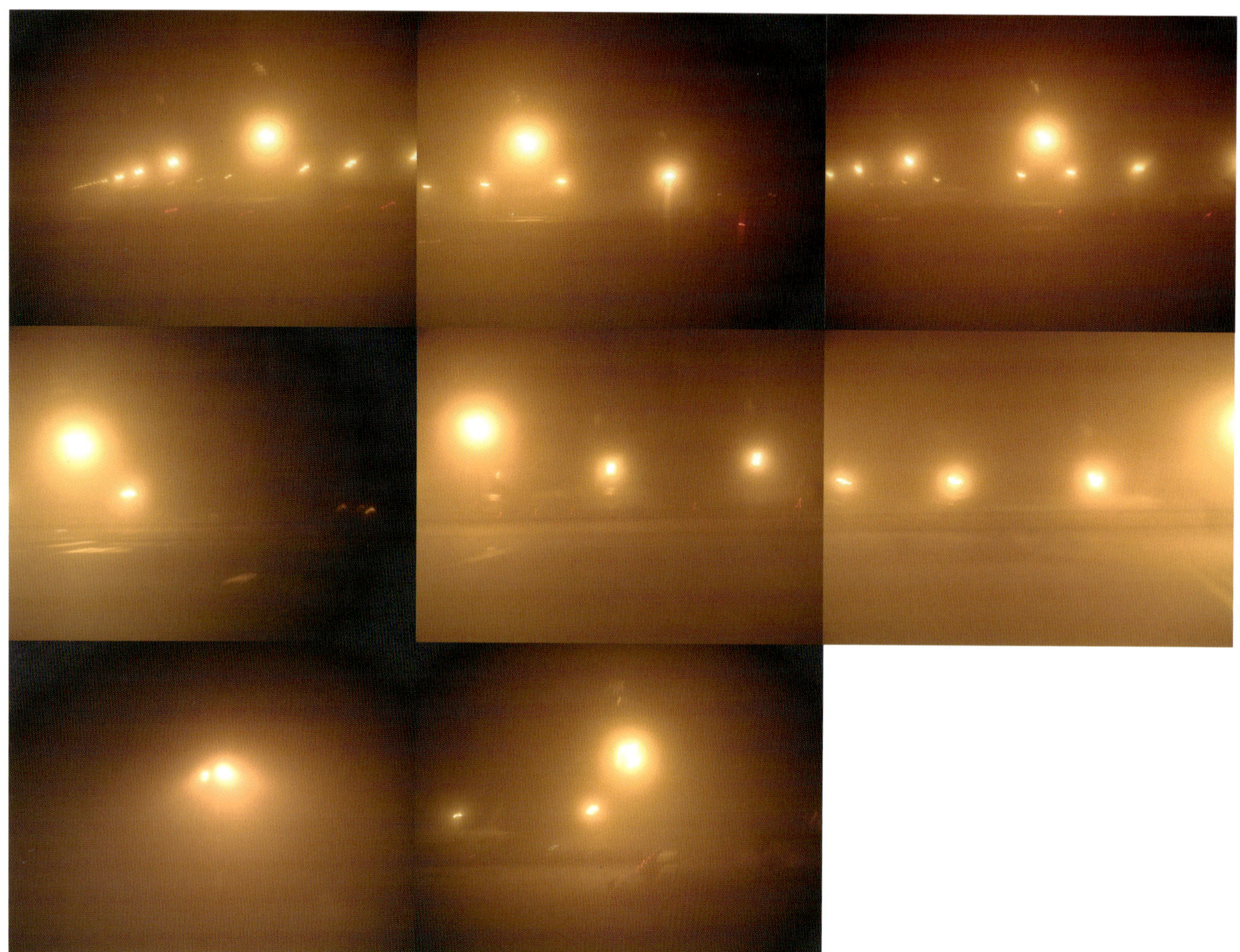

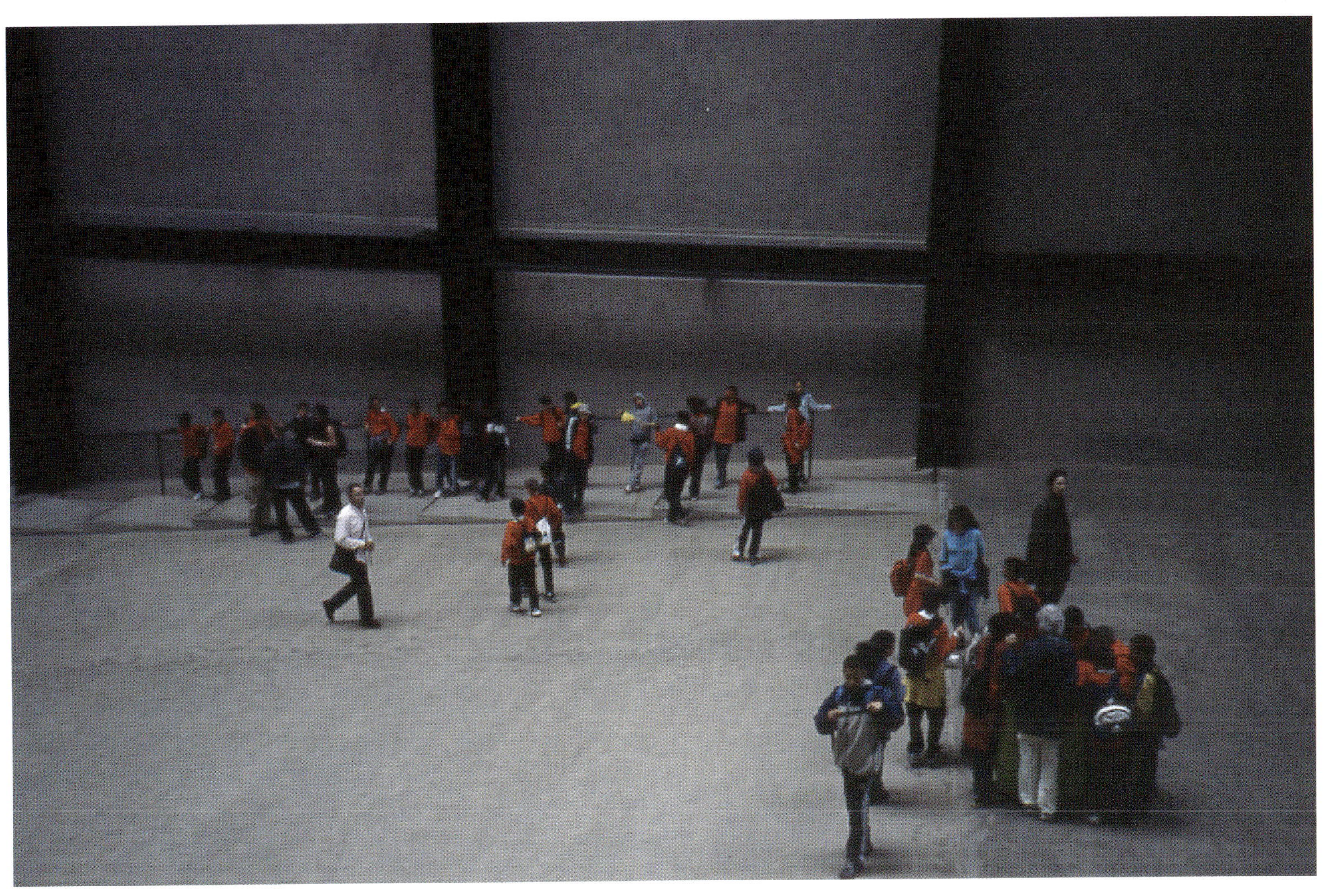

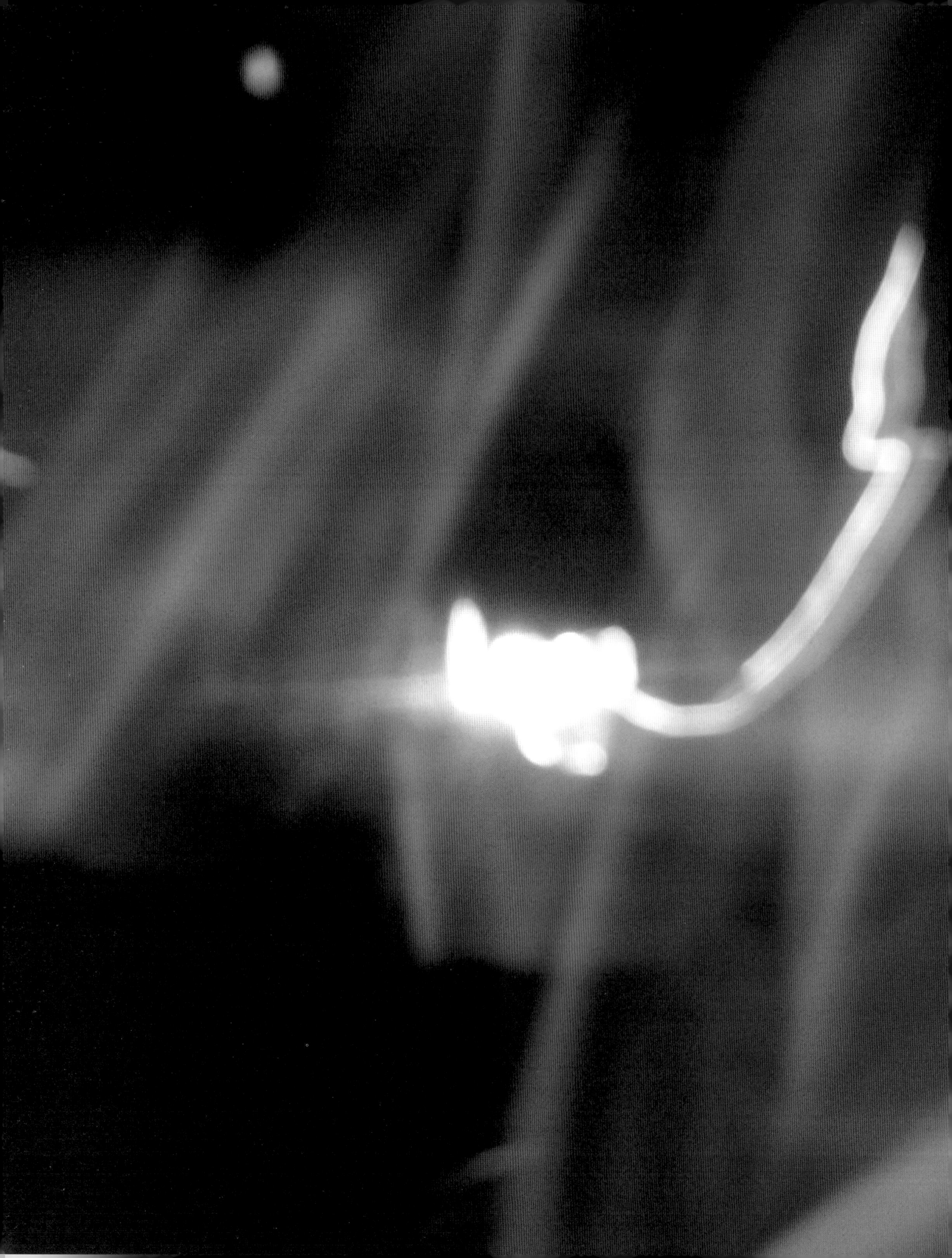

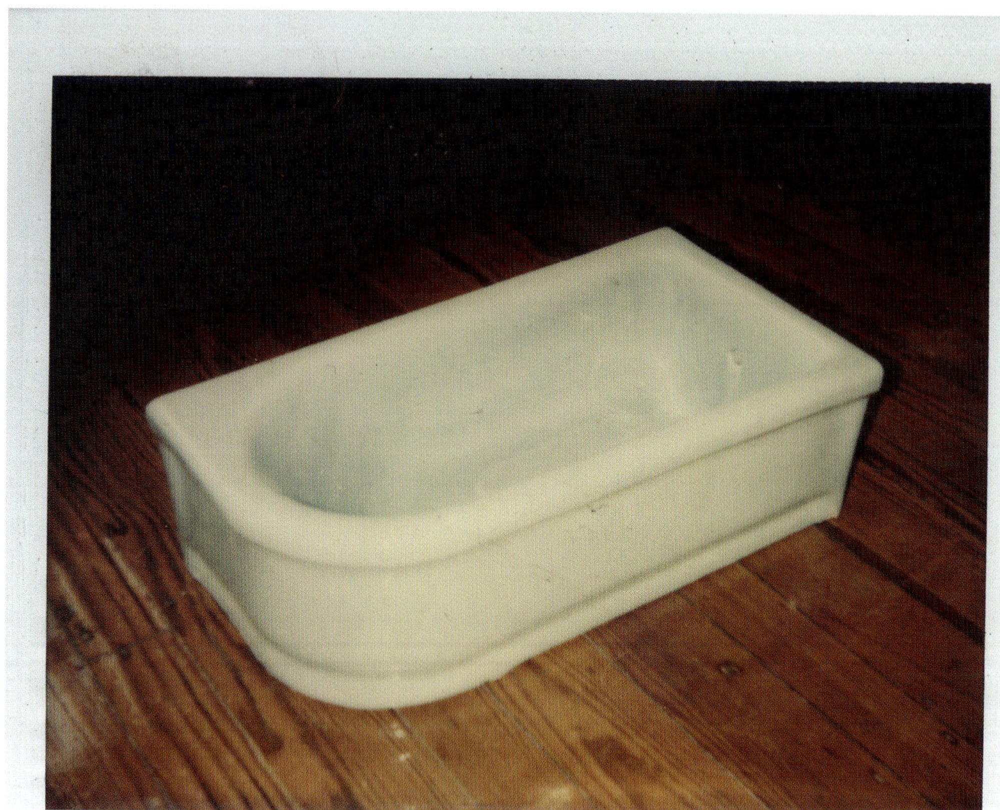

From Green
prototype or scale model tub
ca 18" long, 45 lbs. Maddock

Trenton

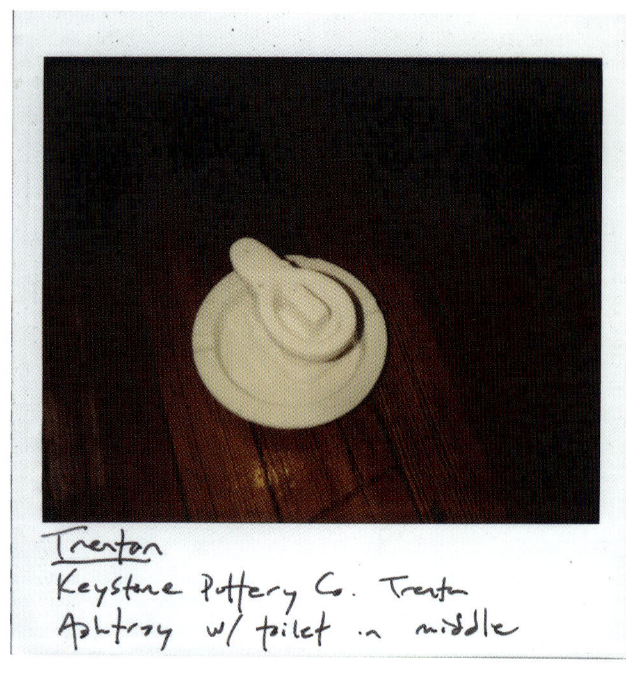

Trenton
Keystone Pottery Co. Trenton
Ashtray w/ toilet in middle

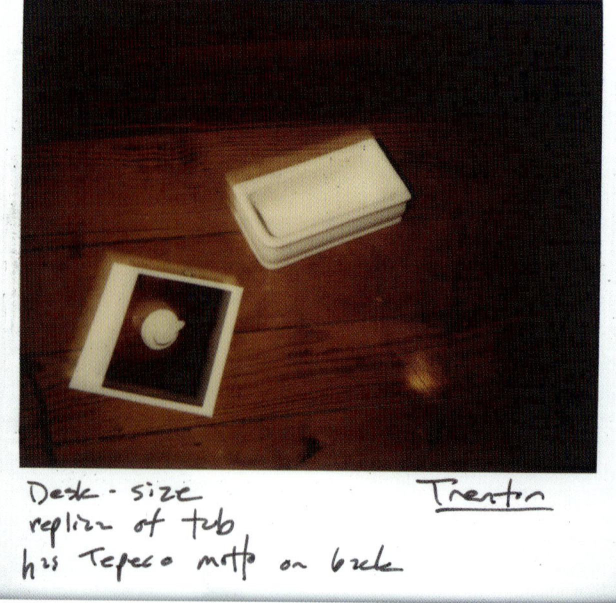

Desk-size
replica of tub
has Tepeco motto on back

Trenton

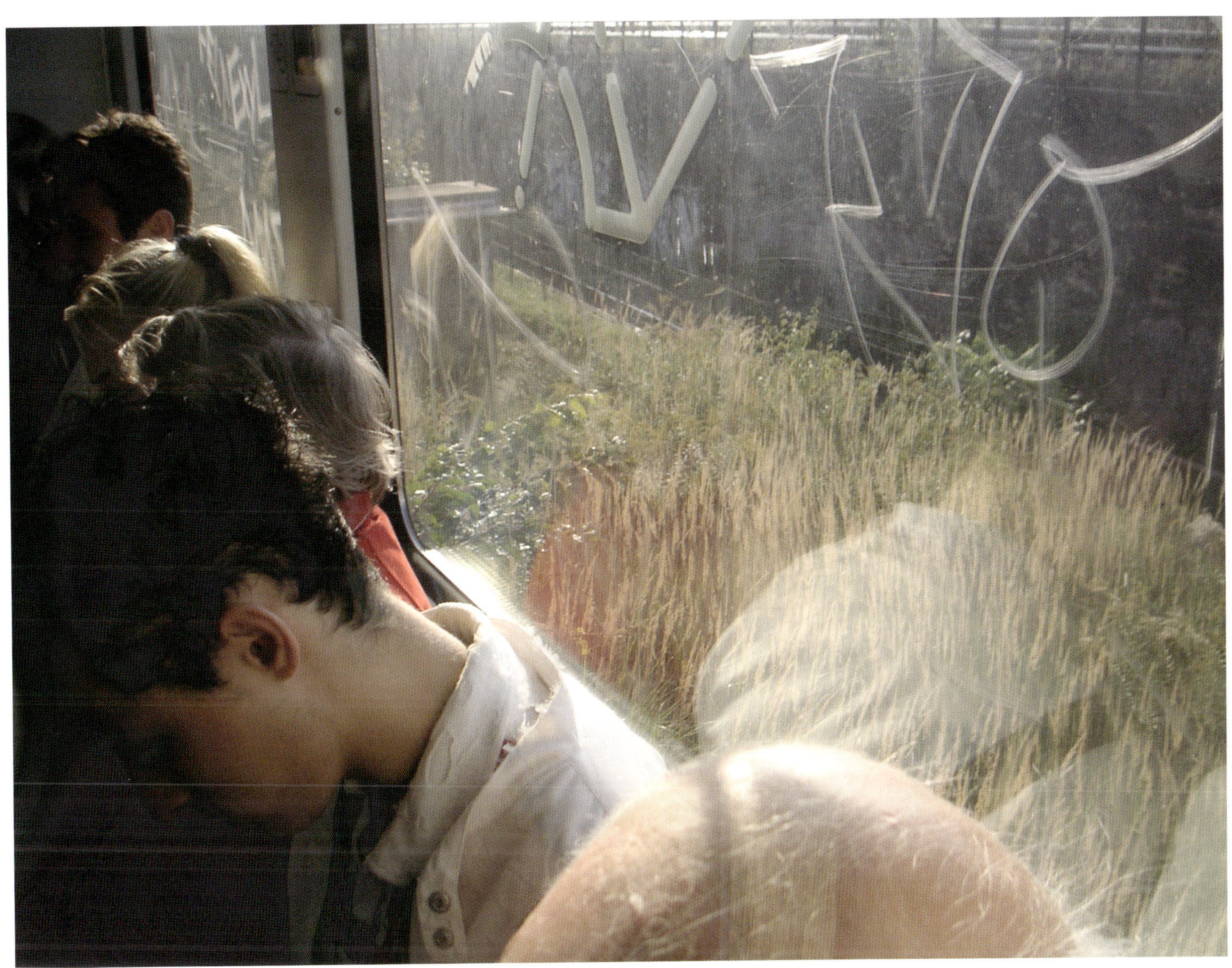

1,000,000,000,000,000,000,000,000.00000000 miles to edge of known universe
100,000,000,000,000,000,000.00000000 miles to edge of galaxy (Milky Way)
3,573,000,000.00000000 miles to edge of solar system (Pluto)
205.00000000 miles to Washington, D. C.
2.85000000 miles to Times Sq., New York City
.38600000 mlies to Union Sq. subway stop
.11820000 miles to corner of 14th St. and 1st Ave.
.00367000 miles to door of Apartment 1D,153 1st Ave
.00021600 miles to typewriter paper page
.00000700 miles to lens of glasses
.00000098 miles to cornea from retinal wall

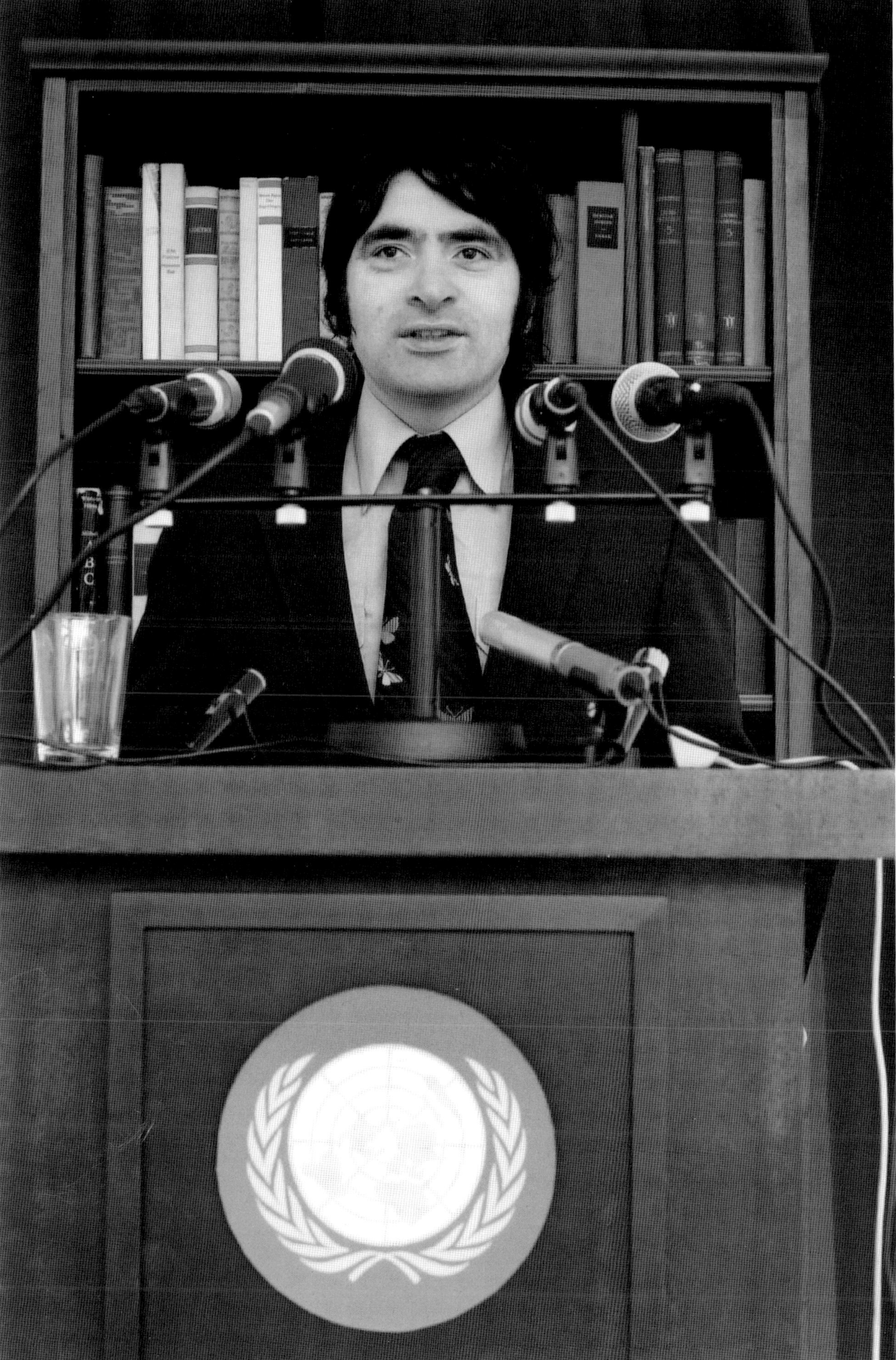

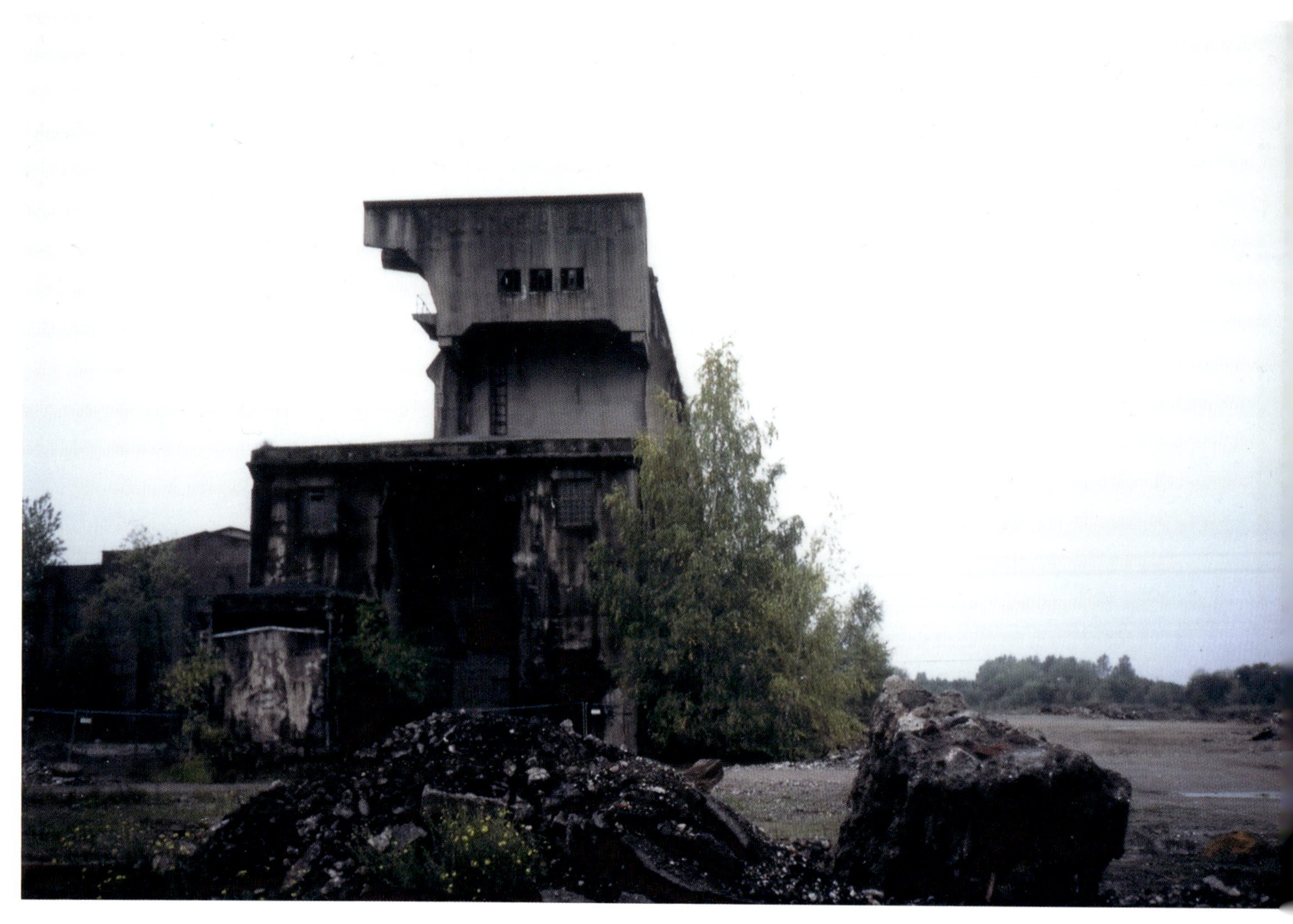

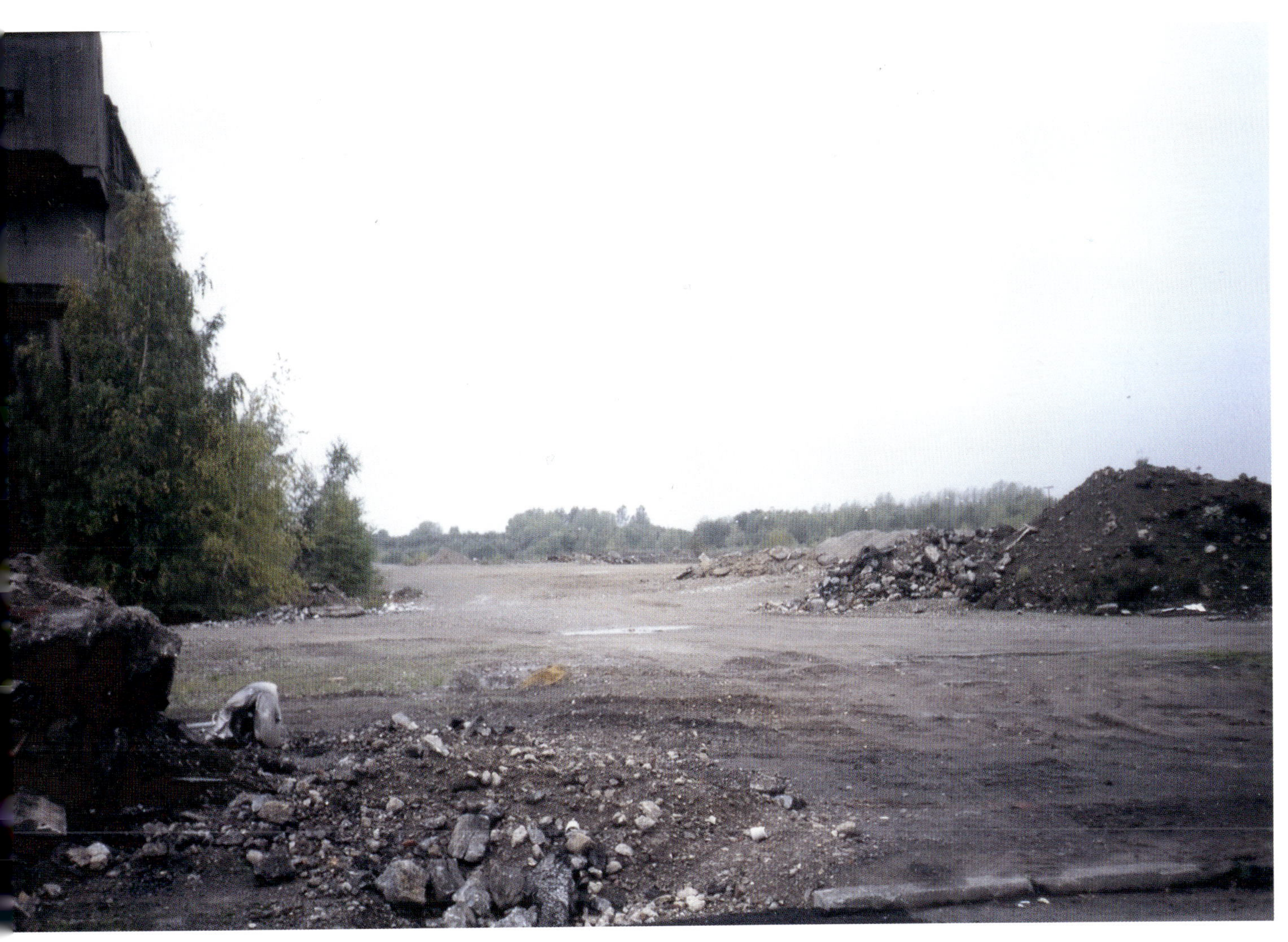

LOWER LOOM LIGHT
UNTALKATIVE
TENSE

INTO BRICK
AIR

DIALING
DARKNESS

CAN YOU HEAR ME?

DON'T TRUST U - TOPIA
WANT THE IM - POSSIBLE

Thanks to:

Mark Dion, Olafur Eliasson, Dan Graham, Fubbi Karlsson, JoJo Li, Doreen Massey, Caroline Nagel, Molly Nesbit, Hans Ulrich Obrist, Philippe Parreno, Terry Riley, Eduardo Sarabia, Joni Sighvatsson, Arlette Feltz-Süssenbach, Rirkrit Tiravanija.